WAKING THE
SLEEPING DEMON

WAKING THE SLEEPING DEMON

26 HOURS OF TERROR IN ATLANTA

The True Story of the Atlanta Courthouse Shootings

SHORAN REID

Printed in the United States of America

ISBN: 978-0-615-20749-0

Subject Index:
Reid, Shoran
Waking the Sleeping Demon: 26 Hours of Terror
The True Story of the Atlanta Courthouse Shootings
1. Narrative   non-fiction   2. True Crime
3. Memoir   4. Trials   Criminal Justice

Shoran Reid's photograph provided by Jennifer Grisson of G & G
Photography, Ponte Vedra Beach, Florida.
Ash Joshi's photograph provided by Paul Wendl, Atlanta, Georgia.

This is former Prosecutor Ash Joshi's account of his ordeal during the 26-hour manhunt for rape Defendant and jail escapee, Brian Nichols. After executing a Judge, a Court Reporter, a Sheriff's Deputy, and an FBI Agent, Nichols evaded capture and terrorized the city of Atlanta. Believing he was next, Joshi feared for his safety and the safety of his family. This is Ash's story.

CONTENTS

To my wife Suparna
and our children

INTRODUCTION

By
Shoran Reid

UNTIL March 11, 2005, I did not appreciate how much I cherished my friendship with Ash and his wife Suparna. Now I do. It was difficult to detach myself emotionally from their pain and anxiety about this day and yet describe these events accurately. As a former trial lawyer who practiced law in Atlanta for nearly a decade, I initially relied on those analytical skills in researching and writing this book. I had the frame of mind that this was a captivating story whose every detail had already been told by the media. I thought I would have to find a creative way to tell Ash's story without unnecessarily sensationalizing the truth. After my first interview, my preconceived ideas of what I thought I was about to do were shattered, and my real journey began. I came to appreciate that this was more than a compilation of one heart-wrenching fact after the other. Instead, I realized that it was a gruesome example of the darkest side of people, and, alternatively, a shining example of humanity that rises above it. More importantly, I realized how deeply I cared for those profoundly affected by the events of that day, and what losing them would mean to me.

At the time of the shootings, my husband Tim and I had both left private practice and the city of Atlanta for a quieter life in Florida. Only a few hours away, we maintained our connections with old friends and colleagues. In some ways, my connections kept me close to the city I will always cherish, and are the reason I am still in shock over the tragic events inflicted upon it.

For over a year, I spent countless hours interviewing dozens of people and pouring over court transcripts, internal Sheriff's Department investigative reports, and newspaper articles from around the country written about the events of March 11th. Throughout my interviews, survivors choked back tears while detailing their accounts from that day. Disbelief is still the dominate emotion for many of the people involved. Reluctantly, people talked about the shooting victims in the past tense, as if by doing so they could distance themselves from the reality of their words. Some of the individuals with whom I spoke did so only with the assurance that I would not reveal their identities. To those individuals I say thank you. Thank you for trusting me. I understood and respected your concerns then, and now. I hope I gave breadth to your accounts and similarly move readers as each one of you moved me in listening. Without your personal stories and insights, this project would have been incomplete.

Although I did not personally know Judge Rowland W. Barnes, Julie Ann Brandau, and Sergeant Hoyt Keith Teasley, they were part of a system and a Courthouse family I hold very dear. Nor did I know David Wilhelm. I can only imagine the pain their friends and loved ones feel every time they think of their losses. I sincerely hope that in some small way this work pays tribute to them all.

All of the survivors of March 11, 2005 I interviewed carry pain that rushes forward like a freshly inflicted wound on even the slightest provocation. The survivors of the worst tragedy to engulf a courthouse and its surrounding city in recent memory are alive, but they are very different people. There are the subtle differences that perhaps only family and close friends notice. Smiles do not come as freely, and when they do appear, they do not stay as long. Others startle easily over sudden loud sounds, while many suffer from flashbacks like soldiers home from war. Other changes are more obvious. Candee Wilhelm, Deborah Teasley and Claudia Barnes are widowed. Dekeisha and Deona Teasley and Kiley Barnes are fatherless, while Christina Scholte lost her mother Julie Brandau. There are those who left the Fulton County Courthouse but continued the work they loved. Several mentioned they assumed that by leaving the scene of the crime, maybe the horrid images of that day would come less often.

As a nation, we can recall what we were doing on the tragic day of September 11, 2001. There was a common thread that weaved its way across the country linking every community, without regard to individual differences. A similar connection exists amongst people connected to the events of March 11, 2005. Like them, I vividly recall what I was doing the day Brian Nichols decided to unleash his irrational anger on Atlanta. I received a call from my mom around 11 A.M., asking if I knew any of the people who had been shot at the Courthouse in Atlanta. Until her call, I had not heard about the shootings, and her question floored me. Immediately, I turned on CNN, then Fox News trying to find out more. I sat on the bench at the foot of my bed riveted to the television screen, trying to make sense of the words coming from the reporter's mouth.

The reporter continued talking while a picture of Judge Barnes intermittently flashed across the screen. It was taken from a side angle while he presided from the bench. Looking every bit the distinguished jurist, he held his silver wire-rimmed glasses in the air, as if emphasizing a particular point. I stared at his full face, salt and pepper beard and moustache, and remembered him being a physically imposing figure. The news anchor described the scene for those who were just tuning in, "Again, early this morning an escaped prisoner has killed a Judge, a Court Reporter, and a Deputy at an Atlanta Courthouse…"

Then a picture of Julie Brandau flashed across the screen, obviously taken in a courtroom some time before the shootings. Her short golden-blond hair, stylishly cut away from her face, made her eyes look calm and her smile pleasant. The same footage looped across the screen on all channels. None of the news stations ever mentioned anyone's name that I knew personally. It never even crossed my mind that any of my friends could be in danger.

Watching the chaos around the Courthouse, I was absolutely stunned and horrified by what I saw. I tried to recall how many times I parked in the Underground parking garage, walked to the corner of Martin Luther King, Jr. Boulevard and Central Avenue, and crossed the street to the Courthouse. I was all too familiar with the doorway where they found Sergeant Teasley, because I routinely made a point to look there before I crossed the street. Then his picture flashed on the screen, clearly his Sheriff's Department file photo, with him dressed in a tan and dark brown uniform. When I looked at his pleasant expression, yet husky build, I wondered if he were married or had children. The news station flashed back to the chaos outside the Courthouse. They were showing the area where his body was found, as it was cordoned off by yellow police tape and protected as a crime scene. I watched in shock as a street that is ordinarily so busy you dare not cross against the light was akin to a parking lot. At that point, my grief was for the lives that had been lost and for the sense of order at the Courthouse that had been shattered. In a matter of hours, my grief would change to fear.

Later that evening, my husband Tim arrived home from work and we began discussing the day's events. He mentioned that our friend Ash was one of the prosecutors on the case.

Alarmed, I grilled him about where Ash, Suparna, and the kids were right then. Tim already had spoken to Ash, but he handed me the phone anyway, because he knew I needed to talk to him myself. When Ash answered, he sounded exhausted. I told him we would talk later about what happened throughout the day, but at that moment, I wanted him to pack up the family and bring them to our house. "Nobody will be looking for you here," I told him. Through his slow baritone growl of a laugh he said, "Thanks Shoran but we're already on our way to Tennessee. We were going anyway and just decided to leave early." He told me several months later that although appreciative of my gesture, it was humorous to him I would suggest such a long drive on the tail end of an even longer day. At the time, that thought never occurred to me. All I cared about was that my friends were far away from Atlanta. The next morning, my mom called to say that Brian Nichols had surrendered to the police. The knot that had been in my throat all night loosened its grip, and I started breathing a little easier.

Three months later, on a typical hot, muggy summer day in Florida, Ash, Suparna and their kids paid us a visit. We had agreed to meet at a restaurant near the beach shortly after they arrived in town. It was good to see them. Ash looked as fit as ever, and I assumed he was back into the habit of working out three times a week. We all were well and together again. It felt familiar and strangely different at the same time. Throughout dinner, we laughed and talked about everything under the sun. Everything that is, except the shootings.

Eventually the uncomfortable topic of the shootings came up. Ash recounted facts not reported in news broadcasts with lawyerly precision. He described how he found himself at the center of a set of unbelievable events. Listening to him, it was almost as if he were talking about someone else's ordeal rather than his own. What I didn't know at the time was that when he talked about the shootings, it helped him control his emotions instead of them controlling him. For Suparna, the events were deeply painful and laying them out for the world to see was something she couldn't do. Instead, she sealed her pain away. It seemed easier than facing the depth of the loss of her close friends.

Captivated by Ash's every word, Tim and I sat motionless while he described the horror of that morning and evening. Usually, I am the one who peppers Ash with questions about his cases, which ends up prolonging his stories. However, on that day, I held my breath while he spoke. In my naïveté, I thought the details I learned that calm summer evening near the beach were the story. I would come to understand that Ash's story, however, only skimmed the surface of narrow escapes, missed opportunities, failed security, overlooked details, and grave losses. Eventually he stopped talking, looked from my husband to me, and said, "Shoran, I want you to write the book." In the millisecond of time that passed before I answered aloud, a pact was formed between Ash and me. He would tell me every excruciating detail with blunt honesty and convince others involved to come from behind the sealed doors of their private pain to share their accounts with me. In return, I promised to write his story honestly and respectfully.

From the moment I committed to write his story, nothing mattered more in my professional life than getting it told and doing it well.

PROLOGUE

By
Ash Joshi

BEING interviewed by my good friend as she prepared to write this book was an opportunity to express feelings that are difficult to share in any other medium. Then Shoran asked me to write this prologue. Initially, I was stifled by my inability to express any one clear thought to completion, let alone string several together in a coherent manner. Ultimately, I forced myself to block out all distractions and focus on one feeling at a time.

I hate Brian Nichols.

On Friday morning, March 11, 2005 at 8:59 A.M. in the Fulton County Courthouse Complex, Brian Nichols senselessly killed people I cared about to satisfy his own selfish, pointless desires. All of his victims were innocent, not one ever having done a thing to hurt him. Each victim left behind many more victims, family, friends, and colleagues, all equally as innocent as those whose lives he took. Not only were the killings senseless, they were committed in a cowardly manner. Sneaking up behind

Judge Rowland Barnes, an elderly judge, and shooting him in the back of the head. Killing Julie Brandau, a defenseless court reporter for screaming. Waiting on an unsuspecting sheriff's deputy, Sergeant Teasley, and shooting him at close range. Finally, shooting an unarmed, defenseless man, David Wilhelm, who was simply working on the home he and his wife were building. None of these people deserved their fate, and none of the fights were fair. Brian Nichols is a coward. In the final standoff with police, instead of opting to take his own life or engage the police to do it, he sheepishly waved a white T-shirt in surrender.

In the 26 hours that Brian Nichols terrorized the city of Atlanta, those of us who were his intended victims hid in fear that we were next. We felt his mission was incomplete. For my family, this was the single worst experience imaginable. The thought that a homicidal maniac was loose and intent on killing not only me, but likely my entire family if given the opportunity, was beyond comprehension.

Can you recall your most vivid and disturbing nightmare? A haunting image so real and terrifying you shudder from even a passing reference to it. Jarred from your sleep, maybe you awoke breathless, heart threatening to leap from your chest, or with moisture on your brow. Did you chuckle at how ridiculous you felt looking at the closet door halfway expecting some ghoulish imaginary figure to appear? Now imagine that monster from the dark recesses of your subconscious came to life, and your nightmare has become your reality. Do you feel that tightening in your chest from knowing that it's looking for you? If you can, then you have begun to understand how I felt the moment I realized Brian Nichols wanted to kill me.

My colleague Gayle Abramson and I were the prosecutors responsible for convincing a jury that Brian Nichols raped his former girlfriend. We failed. A prosecutor's job is to persuade 12 people that the person on trial has committed the crime for which he is charged. The fact that I was not able to accomplish my job in the first of the two rape trials will haunt me for the rest of my life. My failure in the first trial did not simply mean that a guilty person went free, that is a possible consequence of every trial and a hazard of the job. Rather, my loss in the first trial meant that four innocent people were murdered.

I never used to consider being a prosecutor a hazardous occupation, but that was before Brian Nichols. The most unnerving part of this entire tragedy is that I never saw it coming. Nichols didn't seem any different than the thousands of criminal defendants I'd seen over the course of my career. Maybe he was. Maybe he wasn't. One thing I know for sure is that what he did that day, no one else ever had done before, and I sincerely hope no one else ever repeats.

Ironically, I also am thankful to Brian Nichols. For in those 26 hours, I experienced emotions and learned things I never could have imagined. First, the safety and well-being of my wife and kids are my raison d'etre, and everything else truly pales in comparison. Second, knowing as a father and husband that something I did, albeit in my role as a prosecutor, had placed my family in jeopardy filled me with unparalled guilt. Third, that given the right set of circumstances, I had thoughts of killing another human being. These were gut-wrenching realizations. Finally, I realized that my family and I are blessed with tremendous friendships, many of which we overlooked until thrust unwittingly into this tragedy. It is because of this last reason that I am extremely grateful to Brian Nichols. It is not often, if ever in life, that you are part of a moment when every close friend and caring colleague calls to say, "We love you. We support you, and if you need anything, we will do it or make it happen." From California to Florida, and of course from Atlanta, support poured in to all of us. There were people whom we had not spoken to in months, as well as those who were little more than passing relationships, who called to make sure we were safe. When that happened, Suparna and I knew that a great number of people truly and genuinely cared about us. However, I would trade it all away in a heartbeat if I could change the events of March 11, 2005. Rowland Barnes was a friend to me. He was more than that to my wife Suparna, and now he's gone.

As one of the public defenders assigned to his courtroom for more than two years, Suparna thought of Judge Barnes as more than a mentor. He was like a father figure and for her to lose that relationship was devastating. The loss of Judge Barnes destroyed her daily life and filled me with guilt and anger. She spent more time each day with her colleagues than at home with our family. They ate together, discussed current events, shared stories of their children, and offered each other advice about subjects that had no connection to the law. All of that was taken from her in a flash. I was the one forced to deliver the horrible news to her by phone, minute by minute, as the events of the day became known. Worst of all, I felt, and will always feel responsible for the loss of Rowland Barnes, Julie Brandau, Keith Teasley, and David Wilhelm.

In the days, months and years since the murders, many accusations were cast as to who was "responsible" for these deaths. The easiest target was the Fulton County Sheriff's Department. After all, it is the duty of the Fulton County Sheriff to ensure the safety of the Courthouse, and clearly there had been security problems.

As mentioned previously, Gayle and I share some blame for unsuccessfully prosecuting Nichols in the first rape trial. We should have better prepared the witnesses and more thoroughly investigated the case. We presented a significantly better case for the second rape trial. As a result, everyone in the courtroom, including Nichols, was convinced that he would be convicted.

Then there are the jurors from the first trial who could have convicted Nichols. Though I admit the first prosecution was flawed, I believe there was more than enough evidence to convict Nichols. A few vocal jurors disregarded the State's evidence and actively lobbied for Nichols' acquittal, even arguing completely irrational points.

Blame also lies at the feet of Nichols' family and friends. Some of who, we have learned since the murders, had knowledge of his intentions. Nichols' friends were well aware of his desire to escape. Further, there was Nichols' confidant who assisted him in covering up the rape by stealing crucial videotape evidence from police custody. Even Nichols' mother was aware of his intentions. The list of those to blame could go on, but it should not.

All of the people or groups I have named do share some responsibility for what happened on March 11, 2005 in the Fulton County Courthouse. However, the sum total of that responsibility is less than one-tenth of one percent. The remaining responsibility lies with one person, Brian Nichols himself. He alone beat a female deputy to the point of permanent brain damage. He alone gunned down person after person. He alone car-jacked and assaulted countless others. Nichols alone terrorized a city. None of this would have happened but for the decisions of one psychopath. Therefore, he alone should bear the responsibility for what he did.

Although you may never meet me or shake my hand, after reading my story you will come to understand me in ways I never imagined a stranger could. You'll learn things about me I discovered to be true only because of this tragedy. There is a saying that adversity doesn't build character, it reveals it. I lived the truth in those words in the 26 hours I felt hunted by Brian Nichols.

My good friend Shoran Reid and I wanted to present the facts of March 11, 2005 and the days leading up to that tragic day in as accurate a manner as possible. Even still, you may ask yourself why you should care about me or the events that happened to me on my way to work in March 2005. To that question I offer this observation. I'm not much different than your husband, father, brother or friend. What happened to me and my family could easily happen to you and yours. What would you do if you feared from one moment to the next you could be killed, and there was nothing you could do to prevent it? You'll learn how I chose to react given the set of unenviable circumstances thrust upon me. The difference between us, however, is that by telling my story I've given you the chance to consider the unimaginable. A chance I never had.

By the end of this book, my sincere hope is that you will walk away better informed and with a clearer understanding of how this tragedy unfolded. Finally, I hope you realize that many people made mistakes that will be with us forever. However, only one person is truly responsible, and for that, I pray that Brian Nichols pays the ultimate price — his own life.

The names and certain identifying facts about Brian Nichols' rape victim and her mother have been changed to protect their privacy. Additionally, actual excerpts from the trial transcripts appear in this book in their original form.

HUNG JURY

PART I

NOBODY TO MESS WITH

ONE would not look at Brian Nichols and feel a sudden urge to bring your children in from playing in the backyard, or double check the dead bolt lock on your front door if he walked by your home or lived in your neighborhood. Nichols appears as regular as your son's high school football coach. There is absolutely nothing in his physical appearance, upbringing, or education that gives signals he could snap at any moment and hold an entire city hostage for 26 hours. The few public stories from his childhood are not punctuated with anecdotes of a troubled boy who predictably grew into a disturbed man. On the contrary, his former pastor from Baltimore described him as an "intelligent jokester," not as the homicidal psychopath many people still fear. Childhood neighbors described the Brian Nichols they knew as a "very nice kid." So what happened? What made this nice, intelligent kid murder four innocent people? We will never know the answer to that question because Brian Nichols is the one person who could answer it, and he likely would not answer it truthfully. There are many missing pieces to the life of Brian Nichols. Seemingly, his true identity was deliberately erased from public records.

He came from a middle-class, two-parent household in the Ednor Gardens neighborhood in northeast Baltimore. His mother Claritha worked for the Internal Revenue Service, and his father Eugene was an entrepreneur. Growing up, Nichols was close to his older brother Mark. Nichols went to private schools from elementary throughout high school. He was very athletic and earned a black belt in karate. He went to Kutztown University, not far from Baltimore, on an athletic scholarship. According to sources, Nichols was kicked off the football team and eventually dropped out of school. He later enrolled in Newberry College in South Carolina on another football scholarship but allegedly was kicked off that team and left after he was caught stealing from a dorm room. During this same time, there were alleged arrests for misdemeanor crimes of disorderly conduct and making threats. There are unsubstantiated quotes from former teammates in local papers stating that he was a "tough dude, someone you did not want to mess with," but even they were surprised by his killing spree in Atlanta.

Nichols eventually joined the Army Reserve but did not last long as a soldier and was discharged. In January 2007, Judge Hilton Fuller, the first Judge to preside over Nichols' murder case, requested that authorities turn over Nichols' records during his time of service in the Reserves. Judge Fuller specifically requested a definition from the military on "situational anxiety."

Does Nichols suffer from "situational anxiety?" Is he "crazy?" Is he a "psychopath?" His ex-girlfriend Lisa Robinson almost certainly would agree with all of the above. In her written statement to police, she wrote that during the rape Nichols said that his parents knew all along he was "crazy," and that was why they moved him to so many different schools when he was younger. She went on to write that Nichols said he had a chemical imbalance in his brain that was controlled by a demon voice in his head and smoking marijuana was the only way to control the demon. As with the questions regarding his military service, those inquiries concerning his mental state raise more questions than answers.

It's hard to believe Nichols' family and close friends were not aware of the "demons" in his head. In all probability they want to come forward but are afraid of him — even from prison. In the final analysis, it really doesn't matter what Nichols did as a child or teenager. What matters is that as an adult, he assaulted five people, severely beat a Deputy to the point of permanent brain damage, and executed four innocent people. Nichols has shown the world that he is nobody to mess with. Any questions about the depths of his dark side should be closed forever.

THE STAGE IS SET

B OTH Brian Nichols' rape trial and murderous crime spree took place at the Fulton County Courthouse. An architectural hodge-podge of style, it is comprised of the "Old Courthouse" building and the "New Courthouse." The two buildings sit back-to-back, occupy an entire city block, and their proximity to one another is the only design element they share. Situated southwest of the heart of downtown Atlanta, the massive Courthouse Complex posed daunting security issues for the Sheriff's Department employees responsible for its safekeeping.

Built in 1914, the Old Courthouse's ornate main entrance faces Pryor Street. Its imposing architecture dominates other nearby buildings and transports visitors to a place in time when lawyers and judges were held in high esteem. In contrast, the New Courthouse has none of the opulence of the Old Courthouse. Instead, designed with functionality as the driving force, it has the feel of a sterile assembly-line approach to justice. Its Central Avenue entrance holds absolutely none of the grandeur of the Old Courthouse. Even though both buildings occupy essentially the same physical space, each one has a different address.

Knowing which floor gives access to the various courtrooms, offices, walkways, and stairwell exits throughout the Courthouse Complex is difficult to remember and navigate, even for those who frequent the building.

Judge Barnes' courtroom was located on the eighth floor of the Old Courthouse. Its double doors face the elevators and as you pass through those doors, there is a small waiting room with an office immediately to the left. Behind a second set of doors is the courtroom that Judge Barnes loved and deeply cherished. Once inside the courtroom you can appreciate the allure. As you walk into the courtroom, you face a long wall of windows that occupy three-fourths of the wall stopping just shy of the 20-foot ceilings. Scanning the room clock-wise, the next item in view is the Judge's bench below the bronzed State seal, framed against a brown marble wall. Raised approximately five feet above the ground, the Judge's bench is flanked in front by the Court Reporter's station and the witness stand.

In the middle of the courtroom, known as the "well of the room," is the counsel podium and behind it are counsel tables. Then there is a long wall that rises only to waist level, followed by pews for spectator seating. In folklore this wall, which is wooden in most courtrooms, is referred to as the "bar." It operates as a physical barrier between lawyers and everyone else in the courtroom that is not a lawyer, but it holds a psychological meaning as well. At the conclusion of their studies, every law student around the world prepares to take a test called the "bar" examination. Passing the "bar" holds the significance not only of successfully completing the exam, but also grants that person passage through the "bar" in any courtroom in the world as a lawyer.

There is no question that the courtrooms in the Old Courthouse are a sight to behold, but for all their splendor and antique charm, they had one fundamental flaw — there were no holding cells to secure prisoners waiting to appear in court.

REASONABLE DOUBT

Thursday, February 24, 2005
Time: 10:30 A.M.
"I had no idea I was playing with fire."

BRIAN Nichols was the last witness to testify in the grueling week-long rape trial. I watched him display his uncanny ability to eloquently flow from one lie to the other. As I listened to his lawyer's line of questions, I kept thinking, "I have never seen a guy this good." I eagerly awaited my chance to cross-examine him and expose his lies about the rape and his relationship with his ex-girlfriend, Lisa Robinson. I knew it wouldn't be easy and I welcomed the challenge. Usually, I can predict a defendant's strategy to convince a jury of his innocence. One of the top ten tried and true tactics is to bring a Bible and read it during breaks in the trial. Another popular scheme is for defendants to humanize their persona by bringing their mothers into court to testify about the loving, good-natured individual they have always been. A mother's testimony was often humorously sad to me, because they testify from a place in their hearts when their sons and daughters weren't the derelict individuals sitting on trial for heinous crimes. It was almost as though they were incapable of seeing the callous adults their babies turned out to be. That wasn't the case for Nichols. His mother never testified that Nichols possessed a gracious personality before the rape; even more telling, neither she, nor Nichols' father, nor brother ever attended the trial. This lack of family support did not appear to bother Nichols. His self-confidence never faltered. In fact, on the third day of the trial, he did what was tantamount to challenging the jurors to convict him. In an attempt to draw attention to himself, he shaved his head completely bald. In hindsight, the message sent by that seemingly innocuous act is astounding. At a point in the trial when most defendants would strive to appear humble or remorseful, Nichols stepped up his level of defiance. He exuded an air of righteous indignation and wanted everybody in that courtroom to believe that he was unjustly accused of a crime. I continued taking notes as his lawyer, Barry Hazen, proceeded with his line of questioning about Nichols' relationship with Lisa.

Barry asked Nichols if he ever visited Lisa's family. Midway through Barry's question, Nichols turned to Lisa's mother. Before I could object, or the Judge could stop him, Nichols started talking directly to Mrs. Robinson, who was visibly uncomfortable with his singling her out. Barry tried to admonish Nichols to stop directing his answers to witnesses in the courtroom, but Nichols ignored him. After he finished making his point, Nichols focused his attention back on Barry who tried to resume his questioning without appearing flustered by his client's open intimidation of a witness.

Since this was a rape trial of a former girlfriend, Barry wanted to make Lisa appear not as a rape victim but instead a scorned lover. There were facts that clouded the issues and Barry did his best to exploit them. Nichols testified about dating another woman, Sonya Meredith, whom he met at Crunch Fitness, a health club where both of them were members. Sonya became pregnant by Nichols and told Lisa of the pregnancy. Nichols described several encounters between the two women, portraying Lisa as a jealous girlfriend who was threatened by Sonya's presence. According to Nichols, he and Lisa argued over Sonya on several occasions, and it was Lisa's position that he should stop all contact with Sonya.

Sonya testified earlier in the week, and coincidentally, her testimony came on the heels of Lisa's testimony. I hate to admit it, but the truth of the matter is that her testimony was more effective than Lisa's for two primary reasons. First, since she was pregnant, she appeared as a sympathetic, credible witness. Her testimony on Nichols' behalf caused that air of credibility to spill onto Nichols. He crafted his answers as though he was happy about becoming a father for the first time and milked Sonya's pregnancy for everything it was worth. Barry perfectly set Nichols up to testify reverently about the joys of fatherhood. Almost on cue from a question from Barry, Nichols answered, "Right away I felt as though it was a blessing for us to have been in a relationship for such a short time and to have conceived a child. I thought it was a blessing and I thought it was a good thing. I wanted to have a healthy baby. I felt as though any unnecessary stress on Sonya would be directly corresponded to the baby. I wanted her to have a happy pregnancy, which meant if she wanted me to bring her something to eat, I would bring her something to eat. I mean, I just didn't want her to have to worry about anything I could possibly have control over. I felt as though that as a man who has conceived a child, that it was my responsibility to try to provide for and take care of the unborn child."

As was the case with most of Nichols' testimony, the truth was an entirely different story. In reality, when Sonya gave birth, it was the *second* time he fathered a child, not the first as he wanted the jury to believe. His oldest daughter was approximately twelve years old at the time of the rape trials, and Nichols had not contacted her or her mother in nearly a decade. His song and dance about taking responsibility for his child and protecting its mother from any undue stress was just his usual dose of smoke and mirrors.

The second reason her testimony was more effective, and arguably more importantly, Gayle was unprepared to cross-examine Sonya. Most prosecutors have few opportunities to cross-examine witnesses other than the defendant. Usually, the majority of witnesses that testify at criminal trials are prosecution witnesses, and the prosecutor has an opportunity to talk with the witness beforehand. As a result, they know what the witness will say during the trial. That was not the case with Sonya because she was called by the defense. Instead of asking Sonya questions that dictated yes or no responses, Gayle asked open-ended questions. This repeatedly gave Sonya the opportunity to offer more information than necessary and made her versions of her run-ins with Lisa more believable.

With Nichols appearing as the responsible father figure from the iconic *Cosby* sitcom, Barry switched his questioning to two specific incidents Lisa cited in her testimony as evidence of Nichols' growing irrational behavior. Both incidents revolved around her new relationship with Chris Rowell.

"Let me direct your attention to some of the incidents that were referred to previously. Let's talk about the church incident, the choir incident if I can just call it that. Do you know which incident I'm referring to?"

"Yes."

"Tell us about it. What happened that night?"

"Basically, this was a couple of days after I found out that Lisa and Chris were dating. And I felt as though that if Chris felt that if it was okay to date a member of the congregation, then that meant I wasn't as active a member as I needed to be. So in going to choir practice, I felt as though it would give me some exposure as a member just to, you, know, let – you know, I am a member of this church too."

"What was your opinion regarding Mr. Rowell dating a member of the congregation?"

"Well, I mean I just thought it was wrong. I mean, there's a section in the Bible that talks about qualifications for a pastor. First Timothy, Third Chapter. And, you know, it says that pastor should be blameless, you know. A person not covetous, merciful. Like I say, that's the problem with the church these days and that's why we're in the last days of man."

Nichols' use of scripture to defame Lisa was carefully designed, particularly given the fact that the state of Georgia lies squarely within the Bible-belt region of the country. It is commonplace for people to pray as a group before athletic events or boldly proclaim the name of their church when meeting new people. Nichols knew the negative effect painting the relationship between Chris and Lisa as sacrilegious would have on the jurors. I checked Nichols' reference to First Timothy after the trial, and, not surprisingly, it did not support his position in any way.

Meanwhile, I began reviewing my files of Chris' statements to the police while Nichols' lawyer continued with his direct examination, and his questions soon turned to the rape. Until that point, Nichols had been exceedingly confident, but suddenly he seemed even more so.

Nichols casually testified about showing up to Lisa's home unannounced and seeing her and Chris. According to Nichols, after the two men talked, he left and only returned to Lisa's home that night after she called him and asked him to come over. Nichols claimed it was during his second visit that the two of them had consensual sex. Nichols testified that after the sex they argued, and out of anger, he said things to hurt her.

"I told Lisa that, you know, 'You only know about two of the women that I've been with. If you multiplied that times 50 or

75, you would have a more accurate number of the number of women I've been with throughout our seven year relationship.'" He then testified that he left her home around 2:30 or 3:00 o'clock in the morning.

I looked at the copy of Chris' statement to the police, which differed substantially from Nichols'. Chris' account indicated that a confrontation ensued between the men. Nichols repeatedly asked Chris to stop seeing Lisa. Nichols then asked Chris if he was willing to die for Lisa. Chris wrote that Nichols said, "If a bullet was coming at Lisa, would you step in front of it?" Chris replied that he would. Nichols threatened Chris and told him that he was in a very dangerous situation because he had a demon inside of him, and the more he thought about Chris and Lisa together, the stronger the demon got. By the time I finished reading the statement, I decided the entire exchange with Chris could potentially be more of a distraction for the jury and opted not to question Nichols about it. I had no way of knowing at the time, that I would second guess that and every other decision I made as it related to the trial.

After Nichols finished, Barry turned over questioning of Nichols to me. I wish I could say that this was the most prepared cross-examination I have ever done. I wish I could say that I knew what every piece of paper in Nichols' file said, and that I had each written statement, police report, and hospital record committed to memory. I wish I could say that, but I can't. The truth is, I had just finished trying my third homicide case in as many months a few days earlier. The truth is, my colleague Gayle wasn't ready to present the Nichols case to a jury. The truth is, in a rush to help my friend out of a bind, I stepped up to the plate unprepared for the fast pitch headed for my skull. Those truths may be undetectable to some but are glaringly obvious to me now. Regardless, I knew his story was only believable if the jury believed Lisa and Chris were lying. Brian Nichols was prepared for battle, and I decided to engage him from the first question.

"So she's lying?"

"I wouldn't say — "

"Right?"

"I would say so, making false accusations."

"And Chris Rowell?"

"Chris Rowell lying about what?"

"Well, you would agree that for all of this to have been put together the way it was, it couldn't just be Lisa lying, right, there had to be other people working with her?"

My aggressive approach was the right posture to take, but Nichols didn't take the bait immediately. I've wondered since if his cool demeanor had any effect on what Judge Barnes said to us during a break in Nichols' testimony. Outside the presence of the jury, Judge Barnes expressed his exasperation with Gayle and me. He was irritated that we stretched what should have been a two-day trial into four. He never minced words when he believed lawyers unnecessarily prolonged a case, and that day was no exception. As a result, I felt pressured to move my questioning of Nichols along, and there were questions I otherwise might have asked that I did not.

Although mindful of Judge Barnes' desire to move the case along, what happened next falls on my shoulders alone. I passed on an opportunity to ask Nichols one crucial question regarding his whereabouts between the date of the rape on August 19th and his arrest on August 23rd. During questioning from his lawyer, Nichols contradicted a crucial point testified to by Sonya Meredith. Sonya testified that she had not seen Nichols since the 18th. Nichols testified, however, that he had been staying at Sonya's house from Friday, August 20th to Sunday, August 22nd. He offered that as his explanation as to why the police could not locate him after the date of the rape. It had been our contention that he, instead, was avoiding the police. Therefore, either she was lying and had seen Nichols on the days following the rape, or he was lying and had not been with her. Either way, I dropped the issue and hoped the contradiction would be clear to the jury when Gayle highlighted that point during closing argument. Whether the jury ignored it, or dismissed it as irrelevant, I don't know. What I do regret is not forcing Nichols to explain the inconsistency under oath in front of the jury.

A second crucial issue I flat out missed altogether. In hindsight, there were so many questions I should have asked but didn't. It all had to do with whether Nichols knew the police were trying to locate him to arrest him. Nichols claimed that he did not know the police were looking to arrest him. I knew he was lying, but missed my chance to prove it. I did question him on whether he knew the police were looking for him, but he simply danced around my questions. That entire line of questioning, and Nichols' evasive answers could have been avoided had I noticed the information contained on page ten of the Incident/Investigation Report. In that report, four of Nichols' closest friends got together and went to the Fulton County Police Department to inform them that he was at Crunch Fitness on the morning he was arrested. The only logical explanation for how the friends knew the police were looking for Nichols is because *he knew* the police were looking for him. In all my years as a prosecutor, never had I seen friends get together like a band of brothers and turn another friend in to the police. I suspect the reason they took such drastic action is that they knew Nichols raped Lisa and were utterly afraid of what he might do next. They were right.

● ● ●

Friday, February 25, 2005
Time: 6:15 P.M.
"I still thought we might prevail."

"Ladies and Gentlemen of the jury I have read your note explaining that you are divided and not moving in the direction of resolution. As the Judge in this case it is my duty to assess whether continued deliberations would be fruitful. At this time, I need to ask you some questions. First, which one of you has been selected as foreman?" Of the seven white men, four black women, and one black man, retired Navy Shipman Jack Lyles rose from his chair and announced his fellow jurors chose him as foreman. Lyles looked to be in his forties, with dark hair that did not suggest even a hint of gray. With the disciplined stare of a former military man, and communication skills sharpened by a career in sales, Lyles was a commanding figure. His ability to turn the tide of public opinion and influence his fellow jurors proved crucial during jury deliberations. Judge Barnes continued, *"Your deliberations are secret and should remain that way until their conclusion. I do need to understand some things, however, before I decide how to proceed. Mr. Foreman what are the numbers of your split? Do not reveal whether those numbers indicate guilt or innocence. I merely need to know the numbers."*

"Your Honor, our votes have vacillated between 7-5 and 8-4, but at no time have we had unanimity."

"It's late and you all have been at it for a while. I think the best thing to do right now is to send you all home. You are instructed not to discuss the case or do any private investigation of the facts such as visiting the scene or conducting any legal research. Once you have all reassembled on Monday morning in the jury room, you can resume your deliberations. At this time, you are dismissed for the day. Please leave any notes you took during the trial in your chair with your name on them. We'll make sure that they are returned to you prior to resuming your deliberations.

Have a good weekend, and I'll see you on Monday morning at our usual starting time of 9:30."

• • •

Monday, February 28, 2005
Time: 9:30 A.M.
"I knew his own mother believed he was guilty."

The following Monday morning we all resumed our places in the courtroom and waited for Judge Barnes to release the jurors to continue their deliberations. He always started the morning by greeting his jurors:

"Good morning Ladies and Gentlemen. Now that you are all here, I am going to send you back into the jury room to resume your deliberations. It is my duty, however, as the Judge in this case to instruct you on the law of stalled deliberations. The Allen charge instructs you to continue your deliberations with an eye toward reaching a unanimous verdict. At no time should you surrender any deeply held conviction or belief merely in an attempt to be congenial but you should consider the reasonableness of your fellow jurors' belief and faithfully attempt to reach a unanimous verdict. At this time, I will release you all back into the jury room in order to resume your deliberations."

While the jury deliberated, Gayle and I sat in the courtroom

with Nichols' rape victim, Lisa Robinson, and her mother
Barbara. Unlike her husband and daughter, Barbara was the
emotional firebrand of the family and, as could be expected,
was open with how upset she was with Nichols. When Lisa
initially told her about the rape, Barbara grabbed her phone to
call Nichols herself, but Lisa begged her to hang up. Barbara's
emotions and reactions I expected and understood. On the other
hand, Lisa and her father displayed surprisingly little emotion.
I had never seen people so flat-lined in their demeanors, yet
completely engaged in a conversation. I must admit, it was
disarming to see given the nature of how heinously Nichols had
treated Lisa. Barbara commented at one point that Lisa always
had been reserved when it came to expressing emotions, even
as a child. It was a characteristic inherited from her father. That
explanation certainly helped me to understand why when she
testified about the rape, her tone was no different than if she
were ordering pizza. Gayle should have questioned Barbara
about Lisa's demeanor while Barbara was on the stand. She did
not, however, and now it was too late.

Lisa had a close relationship with her mom and the older
woman was fiercely protective of her daughter and only child.
When Barbara learned of the rape she made it her business to
contact Nichols' mother, who was living in South Africa at the
time, by telephone and e-mail. During breaks throughout the
trial and jury deliberations, Barbara recounted to me numerous
conversations she had with Claritha Nichols. The consistent
theme throughout those exchanges was Mrs. Nichols apologizing
for her sons transgressions. As Barbara relayed the discussions,
it was clear to me that Mrs. Nichols openly expressed her dismay
over the rape, and never once questioned her son's guilt.

Unfortunately for the prosecution, the Georgia Rules of
Evidence consider Barbara's statements about her conversations
with Claritha Nichols as hearsay evidence. Pursuant to those
rules, it is improper to present such testimony to a jury because

lawmakers believed that hearsay testimony is by itself unreliable, and without the opportunity to cross-examine the person who made the statement, the opposing side is left unfairly disadvantaged. It also would open the door to witnesses saying anything in court without fear of ramifications. As a result, jurors would never hear Barbara testify to the nature of any of those candid conversations she had with Claritha Nichols or see any of the damaging e-mails between the two mothers. Additionally, Mrs. Nichols was out of the country, and we had no authority to compel her to testify about the things she said to Barbara. Furthermore, it was unfortunate for the prosecution that the jury would never learn that one of Nichols' friends sent a text message to Mrs. Nichols to inform her that he had been arrested for raping Lisa. Mrs. Nichols' response was consistent with the statements she'd made to Barbara when she wrote back, "I know he did it. We just need to minimize the damage." Nichols' own mother knew beyond a reasonable doubt that her son was guilty. To add insult to injury, jurors would never see the videotape Nichols took of Lisa that horrifying morning he raped her. The same friend who sent the text message to Nichols' mother brazenly took the videotape from Nichols' car at the police impound. It's incredible to know that he was even allowed near the vehicle in the first place. It boggles my mind that a police officer did not escort Nichols' friend to the car and create a record of what was removed since the car and its contents were potentially evidence of Nichols' crimes. Judge Barnes was equally dumbfounded by the officer's incompetence, referring to the Detective responsible for securing the vehicle as "Inspector Cluseau," and on some level, I had to agree. In retrospect, I believe knowing all of the background information we were privy to probably made us overly confident about the strength of our case. Nevertheless, I still feel we presented a compelling case of his guilt.

After our break for lunch, it was clear the first jury would not reach a unanimous verdict no matter how long they deliberated. Judge Barnes finally accepted their inability to reach a unanimous decision and declared their deliberations "hung." We immediately notified him of our intent to retry Nichols on all charges. The date for the re-trial was set to begin on Monday, March 7, 2005, less than two weeks away. Judge Barnes denied Nichols bail and ordered him held in the Fulton County Jail. Angry over being denied bail, Nichols was immediately handcuffed and escorted back to the jail to await the start of the second trial.

As is customary at the conclusion of jury trials, all of the lawyers gathered around to talk to the jurors. This was particularly important since a re-trial was already scheduled. The first person Gayle and I wanted to talk to was Mr. Lyles, the gentleman selected as foreman. The foreman usually controls the pace and direction of the deliberations. As a result, it is often instructive to learn more about the progress of deliberations by gauging the mindset and temperament of that individual.

Mr. Lyles was a confident, articulate man who could convince a crowd to follow him anywhere. He had the controlled demeanor and persona of most military personnel, but when turning on his sales skills, he knew how to take the edge off and not alienate those around him. What neither Gayle nor I knew, nor could have anticipated, were the set of unique beliefs and biases he brought to the deliberation room that affected his view of the evidence. Ultimately, his view of the evidence affected the course of deliberations and influenced the outcome. Even though it was Gayle's case, I spoke first.

"Mr. Lyles, can we ask you a few questions that will help us the next time around?" He agreed to talk with us and I continued. "What more could we have done to secure a conviction?"

With the confidence of a trained veteran of criminal justice television shows like *LA Law* and *Law and Order,* Mr. Lyles flatly stated, "You didn't prove the sex wasn't consensual."

I admit I was somewhat taken by surprise at his comment. I knew that acquaintance rape cases were difficult for jurors to believe, but I assumed this case was different. I needed to understand why after hearing the evidence, particularly the evidence relating to Lisa's wrists being duct taped, he remained unconvinced. "How do you reconcile the evidence about the duct tape on her wrists and the medical testimony supporting that portion of her testimony?"

Casually, Mr. Lyles offered his opinion. "I knew guys in the Navy that had done that before. You know, taped a woman with duct tape, but they did not rape them. That alone was just not indicative of a lack of consent." Though Gayle and I both tried to hold our poker faces, our shock at this revelation must have been obvious. I could not help but think that this guy was more than a little detached from reality, and that with him as the jury foreman, it was no wonder we ended with a hung jury.

I watched his lips continue to move, but I didn't hear anything else he said. Instead, I kept thinking to myself, "Are you kidding? Nichols had not used handcuffs or a satin scarf to tie her wrists together! For heaven sakes, it was duct tape! Do you know how much that had to hurt when he took it off of her wrists?" I knew that the case could have been better prepared, but even if we had, we clearly were dealing with some belief systems that were outside the realm of what we believed to be rational. When he walked off Gayle and I looked at each other, shook our heads, and agreed that his view was slightly less than normal. We immediately started strategizing and identifying where there were holes in the evidence that needed to be filled in for the next trial. While we were collecting our trial notes and papers, another juror approached us. It was clear that he wanted to talk with us, but not within earshot of the other jurors. We stepped closer to the middle of the courtroom and away from another group of jurors holding counsel with Nichols' lawyer, Barry Hazen.

With his receding hairline and gray wire-rimmed glasses, 67-year-old juror Joe Wood looked every bit the part of the typical college professor. Opinionated and pensive, but not overbearing or afraid, he looked liked his every thought flowed from critical analysis and deductive reasoning. Wood wanted Gayle and me to know exactly what *he* thought of Brian Nichols.

"I think he did it and I voted to convict him. For Pete's sake, the guy had guns, a couple of them, on him! I think he's a dangerous, dangerous man." Pausing to let his words sink in, he stood before us with his arms crossed over his chest. What Wood said resonated with Gayle because she felt the same way about Nichols. In her view, he was the worst kind of criminal. On the outside, he appeared normal. He was educated, well-spoken, and from a solidly middle-class, two-parent family. He carried himself with an air of respectability. He was involved in his church and held down a tax-paying job with an internationally reputable company. He did not outwardly display the characteristics people normally associate with a rapist. The ultimate irony about his appearance, however, was that it masked his true self. At first glance, nothing about Nichols would indicate his seedy secret sexual life, illegal drug involvement, or complete disregard for life.

Another juror who also believed Nichols was guilty joined Wood. As Wood spoke, 28-year-old Stephen O'Leary nodded his head in agreement. With a break in the conversation O'Leary offered, "I think many of the jurors who voted not guilty, I think they were glad it was a hung jury." It was becoming clearer to me as the two men continued, that not only had we failed to secure a conviction, we were dangerously close to an acquittal. Until that moment, I believed that the majority had been prepared to vote guilty, but now I was not so confident. I turned back toward Wood and said, "Your last vote, was it seven to five or eight to four?" He replied, "I think the last count was eight to four." As the elderly man responded to my question, he looked over to

O'Leary to confirm, and the younger man shook his head in agreement.

There was a part of me that could not believe what they were saying, but I had seen it happen time and time again. Every seasoned trial lawyer knows that once the jurors enter the deliberating room, anything, and I do mean *anything* can happen. Neither the lawyers nor the judge can control how jurors interpret evidence. The best any trial lawyer can hope for is that you have weeded out all of the nut jobs, and the remaining jurors will take a reasonable and honest approach to reviewing the evidence. Based upon our conversation with the foreman and the two jurors standing in front of me, we had some personal views and beliefs working against us during the deliberations. As a result, we were fortunate to have the few holdouts that we did. Even though I knew the answer to my next question, I asked it anyway. "So it was eight to four to acquit?"

"Yes, but there was no way that this guy was going to walk. Not as long as I'm alive." Wood was resolute. We had convinced him that Brian Nichols was a rapist. Now, we needed to convince twelve different people to believe the same thing. I looked at Gayle and she looked back at me. We did not have to say anything. We knew the next time around we had to circle the wagons, because lady luck would not appear twice in the same case.

SECOND CHANCES

PART II

Unfinished Business

Sunday, March 6, 2005
Time: 3:30 P.M.
"I have a trial tomorrow!"

FOR Suparna's part, she was determined that we have a family picture taken. The photographer said, "I think this would work great if we finished up by taking pictures outside. Right in front of the house would be fantastic!" I struggled to be polite to the photographer Suparna hired. This entire picture taking adventure had already lasted for two hours and that was two hours too long. I looked down at my watch and then glared at my wife. She shrugged her shoulders and mouthed, "Smile anyway."

We had not taken a family picture since our son was born, and he was almost two years old. She tried to whisper "Sorry" to me without letting the photographer and the kids hear. I hated taking pictures and had simply refused over the years to actually go to a studio with kids in tow, sit down, and smile for a camera. It just all seemed so unnecessary. I had only agreed to take pictures this day because she backed me into a corner and made me feel uncaring and heartless. Now, instead of being tortured in some random studio in Buckhead, I was being tortured in my own home and the punishment was moving outside onto my front lawn.

"For this last couple shots Ash and Suparna, I need the two of you to sit down on the ground. Sort of shoulder to shoulder. Suparna move your right shoulder a little in front of Ash. Now sweet girl, I need you right here in front of your Dad, and I'll sit your brother right here in front of your Mom. Perfect."

Each time the photographer lifted her head away from the camera, I could feel my breathing get heavier and heavier. Suparna could probably feel it as well. Finally, the camera snapped the last picture, and the photographer announced it was over. The kids jumped up and ran around to the back of the house like wild horses finally set free. Suparna exchanged pleasantries with the photographer as she packed away her equipment. I stood around impatiently waiting for my opportunity to leave. All I could think about was getting to my office and preparing for Nichols' re-trial scheduled to begin the next morning. I did not bother to change clothes. It would have taken even more time for me to go inside, and I was already troubled by my late start. When the photographer pulled out of the driveway, I pulled out right behind her.

Once inside my office, I immediately went to work reviewing exhibit lists and my questions for the first few witnesses scheduled to testify. As night began to fall, I felt comfortable that we were ready. We clearly were better prepared than we had been in the first trial. This time around, we had the substance on the scissors found by the police in Lisa's home tested and it was confirmed to be blood. We added as witnesses Nichols' boss from UPS and Pastor Moore from the church Lisa and Nichols joined as a couple. Both men would corroborate facts that Lisa would testify to for the second time. Nichols' boss was crucial because he would testify that early on the morning of the rape he received a voice-mail message from Nichols. In that message,

Nichols said his maternal grandmother had died and that when his mother learned of the death, she died as well. He said he had to fly immediately to South Africa to pick up his mother's body and bring it back to the states. The call and its contents were significant pieces of evidence for two reasons. First, it corroborated Lisa's testimony that Nichols made the phone calls in her presence and from her home early in the morning the day of the rape. This would contradict Nichols' statements that he left Lisa's home around 2 A.M., shortly after they had consensual sex. We also had the cell phone records from Lisa's boyfriend to show that he was on the phone with Lisa during the time that Nichols claimed to have been having consensual sex with her. Secondly, the actual statements would show the jury how callous Nichols could be, since at the time he made the statements, both his mother and grandmother were still alive. We also added Pastor Moore to our witness list. Though he was reluctant to testify against Nichols, he could corroborate Lisa's testimony that in the weeks preceding the rape, Nichols was insistent the relationship was not over between Lisa and him. He would also testify about an occasion where Nichols behaved irrationally in the parking lot of the church following choir rehearsal. Gayle also had better prepared Lisa for questions she would receive on cross-examination. We remained concerned about her emotionless demeanor, but we would limit her time on the stand to a few hours as opposed to the day and a half she spent testifying in the first trial. Finally, it was critically important that we had the entire transcript from the first trial. Nichols' lawyer had not added any new names to his witness list and, therefore, we could predict every witnesses' testimony. The transcript would enable us to do a thorough cross-examination, particularly when Nichols took the stand. I felt comfortable we had plugged enough of the holes in the evidence from the first trial, and it was time to go home.

Arriving home, I could hear Coco barking as the garage

door closed behind me. I chuckled to myself as I imagined her scurrying from side to side in front of the door waiting for me to come inside. I muttered under my breath, "At least one of the women in my life will be glad to see me." Predictably, when I opened the kitchen door, Coco jumped at my feet as though she had springs in her paws. Suparna, on the other hand, never even turned from loading the dishes in the dishwasher. I was tired and did not want to fight, but she clearly remained in battle mode. I could tell by her chilly reception that she was still upset, but I decided to try to make peace anyway. "Hey, are the kids sleep?"

She slowly turned away from the sink and unleashed her frustration. "Oh, so now you want to attend to the kids' needs?" Her words were laced with thick sarcasm. Immediately, I knew this conversation was not going to be quick or pleasant. "You tore out of here like a bat out of hell, almost running over the photographer, without as much as a good-bye to me or the kids. It's a good thing nobody was actually standing behind your car or you probably would have just run over them and kept going!" "That's not fair Suparna. You know that I had work to do. Besides, you said that at most the whole sitting wouldn't last more than an hour. I've got Nichols' rape re-trial tomorrow. You know what that means." I was trying to remain calm and be understanding but my patience was wearing thin.

Trembling with rage but trying to keep her voice low so the kids would not hear, Suparna's emotions started slipping out of control. "No! Gayle has Nichols' re-trial tomorrow. Stepping up during the first trial because her grandfather had just died was very noble of you. But why are you helping now? I'll tell you why, because you can't help yourself! Besides, there will always be a trial Ash! People are not going to stop raping, killing, and hurting each other. It's the way it goes! Haven't you figured that out yet? You, on the other hand, are not the only prosecutor in the office that can try a felony case. You've had three murder cases in the last three months and now this! This isn't even a complicated case. The case should have pled out anyway. Sometimes you need to say, 'No, I can't help because I can't think of the last time I saw my wife and kids awake!'"

Deep down I knew she was right, but Nichols was unfinished business. I knew in my heart Nichols was guilty of rape, and the fact that he could cast enough doubt on the evidence to get a hung jury did not sit well with me. I felt like he was playing games during the plea negotiations, and this trial had become as personal for me as it was for Gayle. Even though it started out as business, it became personal when Nichols lied his way to a hung verdict. He had to pay for what he did and I wanted to be on the front line when it happened.

I sat my briefcase on the floor and walked closer to her. "Are you honestly saying that if you worked on a trial that ended in a hung jury, you wouldn't want to be involved in the re-trial?" She put one hand on the counter and used the other to emphasize her point. "No Ash, what I'm saying is that you have a family and we need you too. You can be there for everybody else but what about what we need? We shouldn't always have to take the scraps of time you have left over after you give to everybody else!"

I looked at my wife and could see how hurt she was, and that infuriated me even more. I could not help but think that this psychopath arrogantly pranced into a courtroom, lied about raping a woman, and now his lies were causing me grief at home. I could see the pain in her eyes but all I could think about was ripping Nichols' house of cards to shreds and exposing him for the lying rapist he really was. I knew my wife had the ability to understand that feeling, but at the moment, she chose not to. She left the kitchen frustrated. As I think back on the argument, I realize her hurt stemmed from feeling that I did not care about our family. Nothing could be further from the truth, but that wasn't how she saw it at the time.

Standing alone in our kitchen, I thought about our family

and our lives before the kids. We met as young lawyers years earlier, and our relationship, forged initially of a mutual respect for each other's legal abilities, later developed into more. At the time, we were both working in the Fulton County Public Defender's office. I remembered the first time I saw her and smiled in spite of myself. I thought she was the most beautiful woman I had ever laid eyes on. She thought I was cute but young. I was a few years younger than she, and for her that meant I was too young. Undeterred by her skepticism, I eventually won her over.

A year or so later, I moved on to the Fulton County Prosecutors office, while she remained in the Public Defender's office. We became the only husband and wife combination who simultaneously worked on opposite sides of the criminal bar and were employed by Fulton County. We enjoyed that novelty, and the fact that we could point out strengths and weaknesses in cases the other was handling. Like prosecutors, public defenders are assigned to a particular judge and only handle cases in that judge's courtroom. At some point, she was assigned to Judge Barnes' courtroom. She loved the Judge for the balance he brought to her world and their shared conviction to see justice served. When I thought about her Judge, I thought about Nichols and the re-trial scheduled to begin in the morning. I finished my glass of water, put the cup in the dishwasher, and wondered whether she had fallen asleep. I decided she probably had and went to bed.

Déjà Vu

Monday, March 7, 2005
Time: 9:30 A.M.

" **G**OOD *morning ladies and gentlemen. I'm Rowland Barnes, your Judge in this case, and the first thing I want to do is give you the jurors' oath. If you would, please raise your right hands. Please either swear or affirm that you shall weigh and truly try the issues formed upon this Bill of Indictment between the State of Georgia and Brian Nichols, who is charged with the offenses of Rape, Aggravated Assault with Intent to Rape, Aggravated Sodomy, False Imprisonment, Burglary and Possession of a firearm during the commission of a felony, and a true verdict give . . ."*

Gayle and Ash were better prepared this time. They were brimming with confidence unmatched by the defense. Even though this was not originally Ash's case, he had been there for the hung jury in the first trial and at this point winning was personal.

For Brian Nichols this was personal as well. From the time of his arrest on August 23, 2004, anger permeated his every conscious thought. He was angry with Lisa, his ex-girlfriend, and believed she left him for another man who was a pastor from the small church they joined as a couple. He also was angry for a number of other reasons. First, she accused him of raping and sodomizing her at gunpoint, a claim he denied. Second, he sat in jail for seven months accused of crimes he maintained he did not commit. Third, less than two weeks after the first jury to hear evidence on those charges failed to reach a verdict, the prosecution decided to empanel a second jury and try again. His rage grew daily as Nichols sat in the same courtroom, in the same chair, with the same judge, lawyers, and court reporter. He listened to what he believed to be the same pack of lies. In his twisted and self-deluded state, he was unable to comprehend his culpability for sitting in that chair. Instead, he could see only where others were to blame for his plight.

Nichols sat at counsel table nearest the jury box, with his hands clasped atop the table in front of him and listened to the Judge's instructions to the jury. Although he flashed his trademark smirk, he was anything but calm. His controlled demeanor belied the storm brewing inside. He was accustomed to manipulating everything and everyone around him, and his lack of control in this situation was unwelcome foreign territory. His original attorney did not perform to his satisfaction, and prior to the first trial, Nichols abruptly fired him. He retained Barry Hazen less than a month before the start of that trial, and their attorney-client relationship was still in its infancy stage. Nichols skeptically listened to his professional advice and tried to calculate how best to use him in order to achieve his agenda. Barry believed Nichols to be an intelligent, albeit pensive client, who needed his legal advice.

Before the start of the first trial, Barry counseled Nichols to agree to the plea deal Gayle offered. Fifteen to 20 years with a possibility for parole after ten years served would have been hard for any defendant to accept as a "deal." Gayle wanted him behind bars. Since Nichols would not willingly accept his punishment, then she would see his case to trial.

After the first trial ended with a hung jury, Ash pushed Gayle to reduce the sentence offer to ten years, and she reluctantly agreed. Since it was not his case from inception, he was slightly more objective about it than Gayle. This was particularly true when it came to gauging how Lisa would come across to a second jury. She was the key witness, and simply put, he was concerned about her ability to convince jurors that Nichols raped her. Barry considered the strengths in the prosecution's case, and pushed Nichols to accept the offer. Recognizing that some of the people from the first jury wanted to convict his client, he thought it in his client's best interest to plead. Nichols declined their offer, but Barry said Nichols would accept a sentence of eight years. Ash knew there was no way Gayle would agree to a sentence of eight years. She felt he deserved to serve 20 years or more. Even though Ash discussed Hazen's response with Gayle, he sensed that even if they had agreed to an eight-year sentence, Nichols would not have accepted that offer either. Nichols arrogantly believed he could convince any jury that he was innocent and was willing to take his chances. It is likely that when Nichols determined he could not talk his way out of trouble, his murderous plot took root.

WITNESS FOR THE PROSECUTION

Tuesday, March 8, 2005
Time: 9:30 A.M.
"I knew this time she was ready."

"THE State will call Lisa Robinson to the stand." After Gayle made the announcement, she turned to the doorway waiting for Lisa to appear. Like an audience at a wedding, the entire room turned with her and waited for the prosecution's star witness. For the second time in two weeks, Lisa took the long walk from outside the courtroom, through two sets of double doors, and across the well of the courtroom to the witness stand. Everyone in the room was staring at her, sizing up whether they would believe what she was about to say. I didn't get the sense that the stares and masked thoughts of strangers troubled her. I do believe she could feel Nichols' eyes searing a hole through the middle of her back. Even though he raped her and she wanted him held accountable, she was uncomfortable testifying against him.

Lisa knew for some time that Nichols was always embroiled in some self-induced controversy. I suspect she thought with prayer and patience he would change, but even a woman of her patience has limits. She knew that he was upset with her decision to break off their relationship, but she never would have predicted his reaction. I looked away from Lisa and over to Gayle who was in the midst of her questioning.

"Now that we've got some preliminary matters out of the way, I want to ask you more specific questions about the nature of your relationship with the Defendant."

"Okay."

Gayle and I knew from polling the jury in the first trial that many of them did not believe Lisa and attributed it to her lack of emotion when recounting the rape. We knew that when her mother took the stand this time, we would make sure she talked about Lisa's unusually calm demeanor. Gayle also had better prepared Lisa to answer questions on direct and cross-examination. I saw Gayle draw in a deep breath and knew she was counting on Lisa to do a better job this time around. Gayle glanced in the direction of the jury to see how her witness was coming across. She had been on the stand for about ten minutes, and we both knew we did not want Lisa on the stand any longer than necessary. This was our last shot at conviction, and our success, in large part, depended upon Lisa.

"Were the two of you ever in an intimate relationship, and if so, over what period of time?"

"We started dating in December of 1996. I ended the relationship in June 2004."

"And why did you end the relationship at that time?"

"I learned that he had gotten another woman pregnant, and I just didn't think that our relationship was salvageable after that."

"How did Mr. Nichols respond to your ending the relationship?"

"Not very well. Over the course of the next several weeks his behavior became increasingly aggressive and unpredictable."

Gayle strategically moved away from the podium and angled

her body to the right of the jury box, and continued, "Explain what you mean to the jury."

Lisa watched Gayle's every move. Not by coincidence, Gayle stood in a spot that forced Lisa to turn to the jurors.

"Well, after I found out about Sonja, that's the woman he got pregnant, I knew it was time for me to move on. There was a guy at my church that I had been friends with for a while and I asked him if he would like to go to dinner with me. He asked about Brian and I explained that we were no longer in a relationship and that we were both free to see other people."

"Was there ever a time when you wanted to purposefully hide your relationship with Chris from the Defendant?"

Gayle's question was perfect, and I was glad she asked it. I knew she remembered how much Nichols talked about Lisa's relationship with Chris during the first trial. Nichols tried to make those jurors believe that Lisa knew the relationship was inappropriate and tried to hide it from him. He made it seem to the jurors that Chris had counseled the two of them on their relationship then betrayed that confidence by dating Lisa. The truth was that Chris was a youth minister and never had any role in counseling the couple. It was simply another of Nichols' lies that would be revealed during this trial.

Lisa didn't hesitate when she responded to Gayle's question. "No. I intended to speak to Brian about it specifically just out of courtesy and respect so he knew that Chris and I were dating. We had just decided to go to dinner that night, but my relationship with Brian had ended, and that I had made clear to him."

Gayle needed to set the scene for the jurors by having Lisa describe how Nichols' violent outbursts toward her escalated in the weeks preceding the rape. She would bring out the first time he angrily confronted Lisa and Chris by hiding inside Lisa's house to show the jurors Nichols was unstable.

"What happened when the two of you returned to your home after dinner?"

"When we walked in the door, I got this strange feeling that something was wrong. So I said, let's just leave and go grab dessert or something because I didn't want there to be any type of confrontation with Brian driving by and happen to see Chris' car. We were actually right on our way back out to the garage when Brian came running down the stairs of my home. He confronted Chris and the two of them argued. I stepped in between them, because I was concerned about there being a physical altercation between Chris and Brian. Brian pushed me out of the way then pushed Chris out of the garage and put the garage door down. He then grabbed my keys and cell phone out of the car. He ran back into the house and grabbed my spare set of keys out of the kitchen. He then walked out of my house, passed Chris and walked to the condo he was renting from me less than a block away."

As I watched Lisa testify, and recalled our conversations outside the presence of the jury, it was obvious that she had taken seven years of Brian Nichols' roller coaster ride. She finally mustered the will power to get off, and as a final show of his power over her, he raped her.

On paper, Lisa was the ideal prosecution witness. After graduating from Virginia Tech, she moved to Atlanta and completed a Master's in Business Administration program. She worked her way up the corporate ladder to become the Vice President with a Fortune 500 company. She was educated, articulate, and well prepared to testify.

Still, I noticed a vulnerability about the way she carried herself. She reminded me of the kind of women who fell for the guys who were rough around the edges. I suspect Brian Nichols detected that vulnerability in her as well, and preyed upon it. I thought about one conversation Lisa and I had during the period between the two trials. I wanted her to have Chris set off her house alarm just as Nichols had the morning of the rape. I wanted to prove to the jury that he would have had time to get to her bedroom before the alarm company notified the police. She openly laughed at the suggestion that Chris was anywhere nearly as athletic as Nichols. Initially, I thought her response was odd. Then I decided that she was taken with Nichols' physical prowess and didn't view Chris as his equal in that regard.

Nichols hid the seedier parts of his life from Lisa until the morning of the rape when he decided to torture her even further by revealing his alter ego. She was not aware that throughout their entire relationship he routinely engaged in risky sexual behavior. He frequented prostitution houses posing as Asian massage parlors and engaged in unprotected sex with several women. He also never told her about all of the other random sexual encounters he had with women he met at coffee shops and workout facilities around the city. Until that morning, she knew nothing of his trafficking in marijuana since he managed to evade being caught. Whenever she found small amounts of marijuana in his condo or smelled it on his clothes, Nichols blamed his friends. For her part, she believed him to be an emotionally complex man whom she could help lead a more stable life.

His parents were not a staple in Nichols' daily life. As successful business and government executives, they relocated to South Africa for his mother to take a Consulate position with the Tanzanian government, and neither parent had seen Brian much over the previous five years. Nichols did talk to his brother in Florida, but he fought his own drug demons. Though Nichols seemed to want to distance himself from his brother's problems, he still maintained contact with him. In fact, just hours before he broke into Lisa's home, Nichols called his brother as he sat outside her condominium. He apparently witnessed Lisa and Chris enter her home and continued to be bothered by their relationship. While he sat outside, presumably waiting for Chris to leave, he called his brother and his brother in turn called Nichols' friend who lived in Atlanta. The two men talked to Nichols on a three-way call while the friend rushed to meet Nichols. As the friend later recounted, Nichols was high on cocaine by the time he got to him and convinced him to leave the scene. Neither the friend nor Nichols' brother ever suspected that hours later Nichols would return and rape Lisa at gunpoint.

Lisa believed she had become his surrogate family. She allowed him to live in a condominium she owned in an affluent area of Atlanta while paying only a meager rental fee. I could almost see the battle going on inside her mind between the facts she learned about Nichols the morning of the rape, and what she had chosen to believe throughout their relationship.

Before the rape, she reached out to Nichols' mother for help in handling the volatile relationship. She felt trapped by her inability to convince Nichols to move on, and getting him out of her life was not going to be easy. In the early morning hours of August 19, 2004, everything came to a head, and her life was changed forever.

Like the skilled trial lawyer she was, Gayle walked back over to the podium slowly enough to give the jury time to look between Brian and Lisa, while trying to picture the heated scene she was describing between Nichols and Chris in the garage of her home. She quickly glanced at the jury to see if they were still with her but could not read their faces. She shuffled to the next page of her notes.

"Let me interrupt you for a moment and direct your attention to the years before 2004. Did you, prior to 2004, ever share a sexual relationship with the Defendant?"

"Yes, I did."

"Did there ever come a time when the sexual part of your relationship ended but the rest of the relationship continued?"

"Yes. In June of 2003 we were both Baptized and agreed to a celibate relationship until we were married."

"Did you abide by your vow of celibacy?"

"Yes."

"Did the Defendant?"

"No. I didn't know it at the time, but now I know that he did not."

"Okay let me bring you back to 2004. Now after the time when Mr. Nichols confronted you and Chris, were there any other occasions where he exhibited such out of control behavior?"

At the end of that question, instead of moving toward the jury, Gayle moved in the direction of the Defendant's table. She wanted the jury to see any flashes of anger Nichols might exhibit while Lisa testified about his emotional outbursts.

"Yes. On another occasion, Brian confronted Chris again. Chris was understanding and didn't respond and that time ended without incident. On another occasion, Brian called me and was talking about trying to get back together. I reiterated that it was over between us. Then one night about a week or so later Brian called me rehashing this same issue. I told him that it was definitely over between us and that he was just going to have to accept that fact. He said, 'I would rather kill myself than live like that.'

"Before he hung up the phone he told me he was at a train station and that he was going to jump in front of a train. He asked me to take care of his dog Whoadie. He repeated that question a few times then hung up the phone."

"Do you recall the date of that conversation with the Defendant?"

"It was August 11, 2004."

Desperate for help after the conversation with Nichols, Lisa made an offer in an e-mail the next morning to his mother to pay all expenses for Nichols to visit her in South Africa. In her first response, Nichols' mother never insisted or even requested she put Nichols on a plane, instead Claritha Nichols inquired whether he was working or using drugs. She then suggested Lisa contact Nichols' friend who worked in the mental health field and warned Lisa not to let Nichols make her feel guilty for ending their relationship.

Gayle was concerned that the jury might be losing interest in Lisa, and she quickly scribbled a note to me. It said, "How's the jury? Losing them?" Not wanting to break her stride, I wrote back in a similar short hand. I told her she needed to move the testimony along at a quicker pace and have Lisa talk specifically about how Nichols planned to kill himself. I stood up to pass her my response while she asked her next question.

"Now, during any of the incidents were you ever concerned for your own safety as it relates to the Defendant?"

"No, I never thought Brian would ever hurt me."

The entire time she testified, Lisa had been careful not to look Nichols in the eye. Bracing herself, she dared to look at him one last time. Almost on cue, Nichols slowly raised his head and turned in Lisa's direction. His facial expression was blank except for the cold look in his eyes.

"Okay, I need you to move to August 19, 2004. What if anything, happened on that day?"

"It was about 5:00 or 5:30 in the morning and I was still asleep. I heard what at first I thought was my alarm clock. I sat straight up in my bed and was trying to figure out why it would be going off at that time. That's when I heard someone running up the stairs. At that instant, I realized that it wasn't my alarm clock, but my house alarm, and that somebody was in my home. The next thing I know, Brian flips the light on in my room and he's standing over me with a semi-automatic handgun."

Lisa paused and took a sip of water from the small paper cup on the ledge of the witness stand. Gayle had tried many rape cases during her tenure in the DA's office, and she knew that the next series of questions were usually the most difficult for victims. Looking away from her witness, she looked down at her notes and pretended to write a few things. In reality, she wanted to give Lisa time to gather herself in order to resume questioning. She continued.

"What happened next?"

"Brian said, 'Get up and disengage the alarm before it rolls over to the monitoring service.' It all was happening so fast but he yelled at me to get up so I did. He then told me that if I did everything he said that he wouldn't harm me but if I didn't then it was going to be a murder-suicide. He started talking about some demons inside of him that had been awakened as a result of our relationship ending and me moving on.

"He threw some duct tape on the bed and told me to tape my wrists and ankles together. When I didn't move fast enough he snatched it out of my hand and did it himself. He then made me hop to my bathroom where he lifted me into the tub and taped my wrists to the faucet. He left and came back with a duffle bag, another larger gun and some lighter fluid.

"He said that if I tried to run or yell or anything to alert the police he would spray me with lighter fluid and set me on fire. He said that by the time the police got there I would already be dead, but that if I did what he said he wouldn't hurt me. Then he took a video camera out of his bag and said that he wanted to tape what he was about to do. He said that he wanted to be able to masturbate to me anytime he wanted to, even if I was with somebody else."

Gayle looked over at the jurors and they were sitting on the edges of their seats. It was the look every Sex Crimes prosecutor searched jurors' eyes for but was simultaneously repulsed to see. The look indicated the depravity of the human condition and how people are so enthralled in another person's sexual tragedy as to enjoy digesting every morsel of detail like the most scrutinizing food critic. Then, like the end of every meal, the dessert is to sit back arrogantly and judge both the perpetrator and the accuser. Prosecutors understand their role in this performance and have to play along. It is a twisted waltz that experienced prosecutors orchestrate between witnesses and jurors in these types of cases, and Gayle was one of the best choreographers.

"What happened next?"

"He kept repeating that if I listened to him he wouldn't hurt me but that when he let me go, if I escalated things and got the police involved that he would hunt me down, my parents and Chris. He said he would kill all of us. No matter how long he served in jail, he would spend the entire time trying to figure out how to find each of us and kill us."

With one hand on the podium, Gayle raised the other and said, "Let me stop you again. Had you ever in the eight or nine years that you knew the Defendant, ever seen him behave in this manner?" She wanted the jury to understand that Lisa never saw this coming. Gayle needed the jury to see Nichols as Lisa had before the rape and after. It was also crucial for them to believe that the relationship between Lisa and Nichols was over and that the sex on the morning of August 19th was in no way consensual.

"Never. I had never, ever been afraid of Brian or concerned for my safety around him. That morning he did start crying at one point. He cut my fingers when he cut the tape off and he kept saying that he didn't want to see my blood. I tried to talk him out of whatever he was planning on doing and for a moment, he seemed to soften. Then, he caught himself, and jumped off the bed, away from me.

"After, he made me take a shower, then told me to sit on the bed. He said, 'You're going to suck my dick.' He said that was one of the problems in our relationship, that I had not done that enough. And, because I would not he had been going to some Asian massage parlor on Roswell Road and wasted almost four thousand dollars on head jobs.

"I begged him not to make me but he just kept saying if I wanted to get out alive that I had to. He grabbed me by the back of the head and yanked me off the bed to the floor. Then he kept trying to force his penis in my mouth. I kept turning my head from side to side and he started getting angrier and angrier. Finally, he said, 'Fuck it. Get up on the bed. Lay on your stomach.' He then proceeded to rape me repeatedly for how long I don't remember. I just closed my eyes and prayed for it to be over. When he turned me on my back I felt sweat dropping from his face and chest onto me. I opened my eyes to see if I could plead with him to stop. When I went to speak, I couldn't because the look in his eyes was . . ." Lisa stopped talking in mid-sentence. The entire courtroom waited for her next word. Gayle quietly prompted her to continue.

"I know this is difficult for you, but I need you to finish what it is you started to say." Lisa looked from Gayle to the jury, over to Nichols, then back at Gayle. No one would ever understand the black hole she looked into that morning. Lisa had come face to face with evil, and no words could describe its depths.

"He had this just completely void look, almost, in his eyes. It was like. . . It was very animal-like, the whole situation, just like an animal in the wild or something."

Lisa testified for another 20 minutes about the remainder of her terrifying eight-hour ordeal. She told the jurors how Nichols made her shower twice, to wash away any traces of his semen, then made her help him gather his things before calmly leaving her house. Afraid he might follow her, she drove around the city for an hour before finally stopping to call both Chris and her mother to make sure they were safe. To ensure Nichols was not tracing her every move, she met Chris at a random exit off the expressway and he followed her to her mother's home. Since her parents had recently relocated to Atlanta, she assumed Nichols would not know their address or phone number. Lisa insisted that her mother contact the phone company to remove their information from public disclosure. Finally, she relented to her mother's and Chris' insistence and allowed them to take her to Northside Hospital for treatment and to file a police report.

When she finished testifying, I felt as though we were one step closer to a conviction.

MENDING FENCES

Thursday, March 10, 2005
Time: 4:00 P.M.
"I was glad she showed up."

SINCE our argument the Sunday before the start
of the trial, Suparna had not spoken more than a few
obligatory words to me. It was out of the ordinary for
either of us to go that long without speaking to one another,
and I was bothered by it. Usually when either of us had a trial,
the other would come for a show of moral support. Still angry,
she even avoided coming to see me during the first three days
of the re-trial. I took note of her absence but was in the midst of
trial and making amends would have to wait.

By Thursday, her anger started to subside, and she made
her way to the courtroom. Testimony was under way so she took
a seat in the back of the room. I only noticed she was there
when Judge Barnes glanced up and saw her seated in the back
on the Prosecution side of the aisle. Suparna must have smiled
at him. I saw him nod his head in her direction, then turn his
attention back to the witness testifying on the stand. After the
witness finished testifying, Judge Barnes decided to give the jury

a break before resuming the Prosecution's case. He dismissed the jurors from the jury box and then left the bench. Ordinarily, Suparna would have followed him and struck up a friendly conversation with her Judge about everything and nothing in particular. This day she decided against it. It was already close to 4:30 P.M. If she went into his office they would start talking, and she would be late leaving work. Instead, she walked to the front of the courtroom and spoke with Deputy Cynthia Hall about how the Deputy felt the case was proceeding. She and Deputy Hall shared the courtroom often and could dispense with unnecessary lead-ins to a conversation. I overheard Suparna say, "Prosecuting an acquaintance rape is always difficult. You've got to get the jury past the fact that they had sex in the past but this time she said, 'No.' I have to say I don't know if I believe her. What do you think?"

Deputy Hall responded, "I don't know either. I mean look at this guy. I know you can't judge a book by it's cover, but this guy just doesn't seem like the type. I've seen my share and he doesn't fit the pattern. But who knows?" I learned much later what Deputy Hall told other deputies but neglected to tell Suparna that afternoon. She not only disputed his guilt but believed he was being railroaded by a scorned ex-lover. She absolutely did not believe Nichols was guilty and relayed that sentiment to other deputies on her shift.

Suparna turned away from Deputy Hall and spoke briefly to Gayle. She then walked over to me and whispered, "I still don't think you should be involved in this case." As she turned to leave the courtroom, she tossed a passing comment over her shoulder to Gayle, "Good luck with Nichols' cross tomorrow."

It would be the last time she saw Judge Barnes and Julie alive, and the last time she would ever casually walk the halls of the Fulton County Courthouse.

• • •

Friday, March 11, 2005
Time: 8:30 A.M.

Sometime between 8:30 and 8:45 A.M., Fulton County Deputy April Swinger reported to work in the female detention area in the basement of the Courthouse Complex. Although Swinger is a deputy supervisor in the female detention area, at times she responded to issues involving male detainees. March 11th was one of those times.

Just as she settled into the mini-control room on the female side of the inmate holding area, a call for assistance in the male inmate area came across her radio. Two inmates started a fight in the main holding cell. Detention officers used pepper-spray on the two men after they resisted officers' attempts to break them apart. Other detention officers cleared all of the prisoners from the cell where the fight occurred and relocated them into another large holding cell on the same floor. Brian Nichols was in the group of prisoners moved to the larger cell. The cell where the fight occurred had to be cleaned of pepper spray and blood, which was the responsibility of Detention Officer Dexter Jenkins. Once the prisoners were moved to the second holding cell, Deputy Cynthia Hall came to escort Nichols from the general population to a holding cell on the eighth floor to change his clothes for trial. Judge Barnes would expect for Nichols to be ready when it was time to resume his trial at 9:30. It was approximately 8:40 A.M.

After Jenkins finished cleaning the cell, he went back to the control room in the detention area. He and Deputy John Mattox watched Deputy Hall on one of the two surveillance monitors in the room as she escorted Nichols up the inmate elevator alone. Her doing so concerned Jenkins enough for him to comment to no one in particular but loudly enough for everyone in the room to hear, "Why is she escorting him by herself?" Mattox also was concerned by Deputy Hall's transporting Nichols alone.

He left the room with the intent to pass his concern along to a superior on duty.

As Deputy Swinger walked toward the male holding cells responding to the call for assistance in the male detention area, she encountered Deputy John Mattox in the hallway between the two prisoner holding areas. The two Deputies stood in the middle of the hallway discussing the fact that Deputy Hall was transporting Nichols alone. Neither of them knew at the time, that nine floors above, Nichols was leveling a beating upon one of their colleagues that would leave her clinging to life. It was 8:45 A.M.

Chaos in the Courtroom

PART III

THE DEMON INSIDE

March 11ᵗʰ
Time: 8:45 A.M.

FIFTY-ONE-YEAR-OLD Deputy Cynthia Hall, described by many as a good-natured, "motherly" type person, had been with the Fulton County Sheriff's department for 16 years. Amongst other duties, she and Sergeant Grantley White, both assigned to Judge Barnes' courtroom, were responsible for courtroom safety and transporting prisoners. Twice a day for two weeks, Deputy Hall took Nichols from the basement of the New Courthouse to a holding cell on the eighth floor, across a connecting bridge, and into the Old Courthouse. On March 11, 2005, Deputy Hall ushered Nichols on the same route the two had taken many times before. That day was no different, although maybe it should have been.

Nichols, never one to miss a detail, memorized the entire routine and methodically waited for an opportunity to strike. At approximately 8:45 A.M., opportunity called, and Nichols answered.

That morning Deputy Hall secured Nichols' hands behind his back in handcuffs while in the main prisoner detention area.

She led him to the elevator reserved exclusively for transporting inmates from the detention area below to holding cells for the various courtrooms above. Surveillance cameras monitor the detention area and the hallway from the elevator to the doors of the holding cells. However, for the protection of inmate privacy, there is no surveillance coverage inside the individual holding cells. Nichols exited the elevator at the eighth floor followed by Deputy Hall. He knew what holding cell door to head toward and stopped in front of the holding cell for Courtroom 8A. After opening the door, Deputy Hall told Nichols to step inside the doorframe and extend his hands out behind his back. She released one cuff and then turned Nichols around to release the other. In what took only moments, but must have seemed like an eternity, Nichols lunged toward the Deputy toppling her backwards into a cell across the hall. Stunned by the sudden attack, and trying to fight Nichols off, Deputy Hall dropped her cell door keys. During the scuffle, her keys became wedged under the door of the cell preventing it from closing. If the door had closed, it automatically would have locked the two of them inside, and only could have been opened with a separate key from the outside.

Once inside the cell, and outside view of surveillance cameras, the two struggled violently. Deputy Hall put up a valiant fight, but should never have been alone with Nichols that day, or any other day. During the attack, he grabbed her hair, palmed the back of her head, and repeatedly slammed her face into the concrete floor rendering her unconscious. Towering over Deputy Hall at six feet two inches tall, and weighing two hundred pounds, the former college football player and martial arts expert was almost twenty years her junior. In the end, the petite five feet one inch tall, one hundred and forty-five pound mother of two teenage boys was no match for Nichols. Nichols left the holding cell, locked her inside, and took her keys, radio and gun belt.

Splatters of Deputy Hall's blood covered the otherwise drab gray walls and floor of the small concrete cell. The front and sides of her uniform shirt were soaked with her blood. The beating leveled upon Deputy Hall was so vicious that upon discovering her in the holding cell, fellow deputies initially believed she had been shot in the face. In fact, not until several hours later, as she lay on an operating room table in a nearby hospital, would officials learn that assumption was wrong. Nichols intended to exact grave harm but purposely stopped just shy of killing the Deputy. The entire attack lasted only minutes but irreparably damaged Deputy Hall. Shortly after her discovery, law enforcement launched the largest manhunt in the history of the state of Georgia. It was evident that unarmed Brian Nichols was dangerous, but armed he was lethal. For Nichols' part, the demon inside was awake and on a mission of death and destruction.

The Escape Plan Unfolds

Time: 8:48 A.M.

ONCE outside the holding cell where Deputy Cynthia Hall lay barely conscious and brutally beaten, Nichols had to act quickly. Listening to police chatter over Hall's blood-covered radio, he knew no reinforcements were coming to her rescue or even aware of the attack. He bent down to pick up the keys she dropped during their struggle. At some point, the key became wedged under the cell door. Ironically, if the keys had fallen outside the door, it would have closed locking Nichols and Deputy Hall inside. Instead, Nichols closed the cell door behind him and left Deputy Hall to suffer. Using keys off Deputy Hall's key ring, Nichols opened the holding cell door across the hall and emerged from that cell moments later wearing a dress shirt and a suit.

The purpose of Nichols' trip to the holding cell area was to change into the suit his lawyer provided for him to wear to court. Although complete pretence, prisoners are prohibited from wearing prison uniforms to court in the presence of jurors. The legal reason for this theory is that seeing a defendant in an orange jumpsuit could prejudice a juror and prevent the defendant from receiving a fair trial. For Nichols, changing into the suit that morning served two purposes. First, his prison jumpsuit was covered in Deputy Hall's blood, and walking around in it would have alarmed anyone who saw him. Second, the suit helped him go undetected and appear to be a Courthouse visitor.

Nichols knew what he would do next, because he meticulously watched every move of the deputies that escorted him. During his two trials, he learned the route between the holding cells and the courtroom, as well as the names and radio identification numbers of the deputies who transported him. He knew that the doors of the sterile white hallway opposite the elevators would lead him into a courtroom in the New Courthouse. He also knew which keys to use to unlock those doors. Additionally, he knew which key would unlock the door of the black gun locker where Deputy Hall stored her service revolver. He witnessed Deputy Hall and other deputies, over the course of his two trials, store their guns in the cabinet. Armed with Deputy Hall's weapon, radio, and ammunition-loaded gun belt around his waist, Nichols stopped at the door to Judge Goger's courtroom. From inside of the courtroom, one would never know that behind the non-descript walls was a door leading to holding cells for prisoners scheduled to appear before various judges, but Nichols knew every critical detail.

Nichols listened for any talking or movement in Judge Goger's courtroom. Hearing none, he unlocked the door, stepped inside, and quickly scanned the room. Like most other courtrooms that Friday morning, it stood ominously empty. Nichols walked past the wall that separates the well of the courtroom from the pews of public seating. He used the doors in the back of the courtroom across from the pews to exit the room.

Immediately outside of Judge Goger's courtroom is a large red exit sign above a door that leads to the outside of the building. Adjacent to that door is the walkway which connects

the New Courthouse to the Old Courthouse. Nichols could
have slipped through the exit door undetected and quietly left
the building. At that point, he was free and exercising free will;
he simply could have chosen to walk out of the Fulton County
Courthouse. Instead, Nichols ignored the exit, started across
the bridge, and continued on his mission. About midway across
the bridge, Nichols noticed a deputy pass through the wooden
doors in front of him. Sergeant Vincent Owens was headed to
the roll call area on the ninth floor in the New Courthouse
and because of the relative inactivity in the courtrooms was in
no hurry to get there. He noticed Nichols, but nothing about
his appearance or demeanor indicated the bloody beating
upon Deputy Hall moments before or that he was an escaped
prisoner. By Sergeant Owens' relaxed stride, Nichols knew that
no one in the Sheriff's department was aware of his escape.
Nichols casually tossed a hello in Sergeant Owens' direction as
he walked past him. Sergeant Owens responded in kind and
continued past Nichols. Undeterred by the Deputy's presence,
Nichols continued across the walkway.

Ironically, taped to the wall outside Judge Barnes' private
chamber door was a yellow post-it note that read "Open." Nichols
continued through that unlocked door into Judge Barnes'
private chamber and stopped outside Susan Christy's office
door. Christy and Gina Clark were part of the Judge's staff. Both
were sitting in Christy's office discussing cases and arranging
Judge Barnes' calendar for the following week. Everyone on
the Judge's staff believed the Nichols rape trial would conclude
that day, and the women knew the Judge wanted cases lined up
for the following weeks. Gina Clark's back was to the hallway
so she did not notice the well-dressed black man lean his head
around the corner of Christy's office door then disappear from
view. Christy saw him, thought his behavior odd, and called out,
"Can I help you sir?" Before the last syllable dropped in the air,
Nichols stepped into the doorway and she recognized him as the

Defendant in the on-going rape trial with Judge Barnes. Without giving time for either woman to utter another word, Nichols grabbed Clark by her hair and shoved the gun to the back of her head. Trembling with fear, Clark unsteadily rose from the chair. Nichols then lowered his cold vacant gaze on Christy, pointed the gun at her chest, and directed her to walk from behind the desk. He told both women to move toward Judge Barnes' office at the end of the hall. Brian Nichols now had two hostages.

A few feet down the hall, Judge Barnes' Secretary was at her desk typing with her back to the waiting area. Sitting in a chair in front of her next to Judge Barnes' office door was attorney David Allman, a real estate lawyer with his own practice. Allman had gone to Judge Barnes' chambers that morning to request an emergency hearing for a case assigned to the Judge. The Judge's Secretary gave him the option of waiting in the courtroom or in chambers. He knew Judge Barnes had a criminal trial scheduled to resume at 9:30 A.M. and elected to wait in the atrium outside the Judge's office door. Allman picked up the paper from the table next to him and settled in for what he thought would be a short wait.

Moments later, Clark and Christy filed into Judge Barnes' office followed by a man carrying what Allman immediately recognized as a gun. Initially unalarmed, Allman assumed the man was a plain clothed officer clearing the front of the office before bringing a prisoner into the courtroom. When Nichols stopped at Judge Barnes' office door and motioned for Allman and the Judge's Secretary to follow the other women inside, he thought the request a matter of routine precaution. In the brief moment that Nichols turned his attention away from the two women, Clark slipped behind the Judge's desk and pushed the silent panic alarm button. Once inside the Judge's chamber, Allman saw Christy and Clark huddled together in a corner on the floor sobbing uncontrollably. Events began to crystallize in his mind. Allman realized that the man holding the gun was not a police officer and thought to himself, "He's here to shoot the Judge!" Nichols ordered him and the other hostages to lie face down on the floor. Using Deputy Hall's handcuffs, Nichols cuffed Allman and the Judge's secretary together. Nichols now had four hostages.

Responding to the silent alarm alert, Central Control began calling Judge Barnes' chambers. The phone rang relentlessly because three of the hostages Nichols held at gunpoint were the only people who could have answered it. Irritated by the noise, Nichols walked over to Judge Barnes' desk and started slamming the phone onto the desk until it broke apart. Afterward, he turned his attention back to the hostages. He patted each hostage down, took their cell phones, and started inquiring as to the whereabouts of Lieutenant Gary Reid. When none of the hostages answered to his satisfaction, Nichols, with the single-minded focus of a soldier in combat, marched in and out of Judge Barnes' private office. Lieutenant Reid was Unit Manager for the Security Forces for the Fulton County Sheriff's Department and would have recognized Nichols as an escaped prisoner. Occasionally, if deputies were short-handed, Lieutenant Reid would fill in by directly transporting prisoners and guarding courtrooms. A tall robust man with a linebacker build and personality to match, he was responsible for the security of 12 courtrooms; Judge Barnes' courtroom was one of the 12. In fact, his office is right outside the private entrance to Judge Barnes' chambers. Ordinarily he leaves his office door open. On March 11th, however, he called off sick to work and his office door was closed. Unbeknownst to Nichols, he did not have to concern himself that the Lieutenant would recognize him. Several miles away Lieutenant Reid sat, cell phone silenced, and proudly watched his son receive an award at school while murder and mayhem engulfed the Fulton County Courthouse.

Unaware of the crisis unfolding in Judge Barnes' chambers, Sergeant Grantley White, the sergeant assigned to Judge Barnes' courtroom, was on his way back to the Judge's chambers after getting breakfast. By coincidence, he found himself on the same elevator as Prosecutor Joshi. As Joshi exited the elevator at the seventh floor Sergeant White commented, "Nichols knows he's going down." Sergeant White remained on the elevator and continued to the eighth floor. With his side arm strapped in his belt, he casually carried a white Styrofoam container as he bypassed the main entrance doors to Judge Barnes' courtroom. The Judge was in the midst of a hearing before resuming the Nichols case and walking through the courtroom carrying food would have been unprofessional, so Sergeant White used Judge Barnes' private chamber entrance instead.

As Sergeant White opened the unlocked door to Judge Barnes' chambers, Nichols sprang from behind the door, pinned him against the wall, and put a gun to his head. White surveyed the area, tried to assess the situation and reached for his gun. Nichols said, "Don't try it old man. I've got nothing to lose." Leaving the Sergeant's breakfast strewn in the corner by the door, Nichols forced him to hand over his gun. He then marched the Sergeant toward the office with the other hostages. Nichols now had his fifth hostage.

Meanwhile, the hostages felt helpless but believed that Sergeant White would save them. No sooner had the thought crossed Allman's mind than he heard a scuffle just beyond the door. Relieved, the Judge's Secretary said, "Good, Grantley's here. We'll be okay." As Sergeant White walked through the Judge's office door with his hands in the air, followed by Nichols holding a gun to his back, more angst and terror gripped the room. Allman thought to himself that White had been the last line of defense, and they all were now completely at the whim of a desperate man.

Without warning, Sergeant White clutched his chest and began gasping for air. It appeared that the stress of the situation forced the 60-year-old Sergeant to suffer a heart attack. In reality, his collapse to the floor and chest clutching were the performance of a lifetime. Sergeant White tried to alert his colleagues to the situation unfolding in Judge Barnes' chambers by faking a heart attack. When he fell to the floor, he pushed the silent panic alarm button under the Judge's desk and hoped help would arrive shortly. Instead, Central Control continued to try to reach the office by telephone without sending personnel to Judge Barnes' chambers to determine the reason for the second distress signal.

Nichols walked over to Deputy White and snatched the tie from around his neck. Disgusted when he realized that it was only a clip-on tie, he threw it to the floor. With a tear-stained face, the Judge's Secretary pleaded with Nichols to leave the Jamaican-born deputy alone. "He has a heart condition. He needs help. Please leave him. Please." Apparently, Nichols wanted a tie to complete his disguise as a visitor to the Courthouse. He bypassed the pleading Secretary, bent over Allman and yanked at the lawyer's silk tie, but abandoned the effort when it did not slip off easily. Nichols turned to the Judge's Secretary and inquired about the Judge's whereabouts. She responded, "He's in the courtroom. They're all in the courtroom."

By this time, the other phones in the office were ringing incessantly, and welfare check signals were coming across the deputies' radios. Irritated by the interruptions, Nichols fumbled with the buttons on Sergeant White's radio saying, "How do you work this thing?" Nichols did not realize that randomly pressing the keys on the radio caused ear-splitting feedback on other department radios throughout the Courthouse. He continued until he figured out how to respond to the calls on Sergeant White's radio. With chilling calm and control, he responded, "Unit 58 Sergeant Grantley White responding." Unsure whether help for the hostages was on the way, Nichols locked Sergeant White in a closet and then left the remaining hostages in the Judge's office. He left the office for the last time. Moments later, the hostages heard the horrific sound of gunshots echo off the walls in the distance. Paralyzed, they feared the worst and anxiously awaited rescue.

· · ·

Time: 8:55 A.M.

Nichols could have escaped with his only victim being Deputy Hall. However, his plan as later unfolded was to kill the court personnel working on his trial. First Judge Barnes, then the Prosecutors, then Julie Brandau, and anyone else who stood in his way.

Unaware of Nichols' murderous intentions, Judge Barnes had scheduled an 8:30 A.M. hearing in an unrelated civil case with attorney Richard Robbins and his opposing counsel. During the hearing, both Robbins and Judge Barnes were visibly bored and doodled on their legal pads struggling to stay engaged. Without warning, Judge Barnes suddenly interrupted opposing counsel's long-winded soliloquy. *"Excuse me Counselor but I want to make sure that my ears are not deceiving me."* With a slight head nod and wink in Robbins' direction, he continued, *"Madame Court Reporter please read aloud the last few lines of Counselor's argument. If I'm not mistaken, he just cited a case argued last year by our esteemed colleague, Mr. Robbins."* Judge Barnes rarely passed on an opportunity to make a joke or get a laugh, even during serious proceedings. Even Julie got the joke and chuckled to herself as she flipped through the steno typed paper hanging to the floor from the back of her recording machine. Finding the reference the Judge wanted, Julie light-heartedly read the lines aloud. Judge Barnes smiled, took a sip from his coffee mug, and leaned back in his chair, momentarily satisfied with his efforts. As he gingerly leaned forward to place his coffee mug down, he looked at Robbins and said, *"I love to be in the company of greatness."*

Suddenly, a loud unfamiliar noise shattered the jovial air which moments before had filled the courtroom. Initially, it sounded like someone had thrown a flagpole or an exhibit easel to the floor. Robbins looked at Judge Barnes and forced his brain to register the image before him. The Judge was lifeless and slumped over to the right in his chair. A small trickle of blood streamed down from behind his left ear. Brian Nichols shot Judge Barnes in the back of the head at close range.

Nichols then looked toward his next target seated at the prosecutor's table. The two men locked eyes. Nichols pointed the gun in that direction and aimed for Robbins' chest. Fractions of seconds passed as hurried thoughts moved through each man's mind. Nichols initially believed Ash to be the male figure at the prosecutor's table and intended to kill him next. For Robbins, the thoughts racing through his mind came in rapid-fire succession, as time seemed to stand still. "This guy is going to kill the Prosecutor next, and I am sitting at the prosecutor's table!" A millisecond passed. Robbins could feel the gunman's calm rage. His posture was purposeful and determined. He knew no amount of persuasion would convince this man to alter his plan of action. Another millisecond passed. Robbins bolted from his seat and through the small wooden swing doors that sealed the well of the courtroom from the public. Things again started to happen in real time. Running for his life, he thought to himself, "I will not be a full target. He'll just have to shoot me in the back!"

Realizing that the man running from the courtroom was not Ash, Nichols turned the gun away from Robbins and took aim at his next victim, Julie Brandau. Julie's thought process mirrored Robbins', and she stood to run away. She did not make it past her chair before Nichols shot her in the back of the head as well. Unlike Judge Barnes, who fell silently without warning, Julie knew that she was trying to flee from death. The bullet that sliced through Julie and ended her life, also hit Judge Barnes' staff attorney, Lynette Davis, in the arm. As Davis instinctively reached for her injured arm, Julie's lifeless body fell onto her. Davis' screams of pain and fear pierced the air and followed Nichols as he fled the courtroom only seconds behind Robbins.

Why shoot the Judge or the Court Reporter? This was a jury trial, and the jurors were to decide his fate. Judge Barnes and Julie were only performing their duties. Ironically, Nichols killed the one person who would have prevented his incarceration in the first place. Unbeknownst to Nichols, Judge Barnes had spoken to his daughter earlier that morning and commented how he wished Nichols had opted for a bench trial, because if he had, he would have acquitted him.

Nichols had been a jail escapee for less than 15 minutes. In that time, he committed nine felonies by brutally beating Deputy Hall, taking five hostages, killing two people, and wounding another. It was 8:55 A.M.

INTUITION

Time: 8:56 A.M.

EVERY Friday morning the investigators of the Fulton
County District Attorney's Office, most of whom are
former police officers, have a department meeting to
recap the events of the prior week. Typically, the meetings are
held in the conference room on the seventh floor located directly
below Judge Barnes' courtroom. Tracy Baker, Investigator for
the Major Case Unit, attended the meeting that morning as he
usually did.

Baker took a seat and prepared to hear his colleagues go on
and on about routine matters like locating witnesses and serving
subpoenas. Others spoke only when necessary and then said only
what was relevant. Baker usually fell into the latter category and
that day was no different. Midway through the meeting, Cindy
Williamson took the floor. Williamson was a 15-year veteran
of the Sex Crimes Investigative Unit. Years before as a social
worker, Williamson traveled alone into dangerous and volatile
situations. Out of necessity, she learned to read people and their
non-verbal body language cues. Although she can be soft spoken
at times, she is unafraid to speak her mind when necessary.

Baker and Williamson had a mutual respect for each other after working together for a number of years and often consulted one another on various cases. Baker listened as Williamson recounted the highlights of the prior week in the Nichols rape re-trial. She reminded the room of the specifics of the case, namely that it was an acquaintance rape at gunpoint. She recalled for her colleagues that the first case ended in a hung jury and that this was the end of the second trial. She also told them that she expected the Defendant to take the stand later in the day. Baker, intrigued by Williamson's case, learned during his years as a street cop to listen and follow his instincts. Though nothing she said alarmed him, she had his attention.

She described how on Wednesday of that week, one of the guards noticed Nichols was walking "funny" and wanted to know why. The deputy requested Nichols be searched before being transported back to the jail. The deputies found a pair of shanks in his shoes which had apparently been there all day. Nichols' story was that he needed them for arch support. Deputies did not believe him, and filled out the appropriate paperwork detailing the discovery of the shanks in Nichols' possession. Judge Barnes called a meeting with all of the lawyers involved to tell them of the discovery. Williamson said the Judge's plan was to request additional security for the reading of the verdict. With nothing else to report, Williamson took her seat. As the rest of the room moved on to the next investigator and the next case, Baker's thoughts lingered for a moment longer on Williamson. He normally found her unaffected delivery of gruesome details or tragic events fascinating, and yet that day, something was different. He could not pinpoint what triggered an alarm in his mind and reluctantly dismissed the thought. He tuned back into the meeting as the Commander adjourned for the morning. It was 8:56 A.M.

THE DAY OF RECKONING

Time: 8:57 A.M.
"I thought it would be like any other trial Friday."

I PARKED my car in the Underground parking lot and headed toward the Old Courthouse. In my mind, I kept hearing the conversation I wanted to have with Gayle about the Nichols trial. After leaving a message on her answering machine the night before, I knew she would not return my call before morning. I waited for the light to change at the corner of Martin Luther King, Jr. Boulevard and Pryor Street and chuckled to myself at Gayle's aversion to the telephone. She was notorious for not answering her phone or even returning calls. It really didn't matter that much to me, because what I wanted to say to her could wait. I knew Gayle well enough that the conversation would not be long, and she would probably agree with my idea.

I walked into the building, flashed my county issued ID badge, and bypassed security. That badge was definitely one of the benefits of being a prosecutor. With it, I usually didn't wait in Courthouse security lines and sometimes it helped me avoid a speeding ticket or two. The elevator lobby area of the Courthouse was humming with the usual buzz, though Fridays are light in terms of foot traffic through the building. I got on the elevator and pressed seven. It stopped on the second floor, and Deputy Grantley White stepped on carrying his breakfast from the Courthouse cafeteria.

Having known Deputy White for several years, we always made small talk. "Hey Deputy White. Ready for Nichols today?" He responded that he was and before the two of us could say much more, the elevator doorbell softly sounded signaling our arrival to the seventh floor. I moved away from the wall as the doors parted and told Deputy White I would see him in a few minutes. As I stepped off the elevator and before the doors closed, he called out to me in his thick Jamaican accent, "Nichols knows he's going down." I lingered for a few moments at the closed elevator doors and wondered what prompted his comment. Unable to figure out why he said it, I dismissed the thought and turned my attention back to the conversation I needed to have with Gayle.

She and I were Assistant Deputy District Attorneys assigned to the Crimes Against Women and Children division of the Fulton County District Attorney's office. Most people refer to our division as the "Sex Crimes Unit" because we primarily prosecute crimes that involve sex. After a couple of months in the Unit, I was unable to look at people the same way. The atrocities human beings inflict upon one another never ceased to amaze or disgust me, but it certainly meant job security. As a result, Sex Crimes has a very demanding trial schedule, second only to the County's most demanding division, Homicide. I left that division a year or so before, and despite my disgust with the Sex Crimes Unit, I never regretted the decision to leave Homicide.

Since Gayle and I had substantial courtroom experience, and complementary courtroom styles, we often found ourselves working together on cases. Frequently, we would consult one another on trial strategies or share in the prosecution of a

particularly interesting case. Another dubious distinction
we shared was routinely arriving to work late. Our boss, Paul
Howard, strictly enforced tardiness and attendance rules and
frowned upon those who did not adhere to them. We all tried
to find ways to circumvent the rules and not get caught being
late. Gayle and I would outsmart the system and have a little fun
in the process by leaving our office lights on at night before we
left the building. We assumed that if the office lights were on
in the morning, Mr. Howard and everyone else would think we
were present in the building, just not at our desks. It became
a challenge between us to see who could arrive at the office
first and turn the other person's light out. In retrospect, the
games we played seem silly. On the other hand, when you are
face-to-face with deplorable displays of human indecency on a
daily basis, light-hearted office games like this were a welcome
reprieve.

On this morning, neither of us was late. I walked past my
office and went directly to Gayle's office. She was already sitting
at her desk with papers spread before her preparing for trial. We
agreed that testimony would take most of the morning, but we
would probably get to closing arguments on that day as well.

I walked in and got right to the point. "I've got an idea for
the closing argument. I've been thinking about it since last
night, when you didn't return my call." She looked at me with a
slight smile and a small shrug of her shoulders, as if to say, "You
knew I wouldn't. "

I knew the stakes were higher for this second trial because
Gayle was determined to see justice delivered. She listened to
Lisa Robinson, the rape victim, describe in graphic detail how
Nichols had taken her hostage at gunpoint and raped her at
will, while videotaping parts of the ordeal. Gayle was appalled
at the way Nichols nonchalantly sat with a smug grin on his face
during the first trial as witness after witness testified against him.
She had been the only one throughout that trial to meet his

icy stare with one equally as strong. Moreover, her grandfather passed away on the same day the first trial began. Was she at her best for that first trial? If she answered that question honestly, the answer would be no. However, she was determined to get everything right this time around, and nothing was going to slip by her. Her focus and resolve made her open to hear anything I had to say, because nothing would distract her.

I leaned against the doorway of her office and she looked up from the papers on her desk but did not put the pen down. It was her subtle cue for me to make it quick. "I think we need to visually illustrate the disparity in the amount of evidence the State presented and what the Defense has presented. Nichols' story during the first trial was that everybody was lying and the sex was consensual. That's a much harder sell when the jurors can visualize the number of witnesses on each side and have the pertinent parts of their testimony highlighted. You should write each witnesses' name on the board along with some key words from their testimony. That will force the jury to see the evidence from our perspective."

I looked down at the notes on her desk and realized they were for Nichols' cross-examination. I thought about our conversation from a few days before when she informed me that she would question Nichols during the second trial. I conducted his cross-examination during the first trial, and the trial lawyer in me wanted to finish the job. I wanted to expose Nichols for the liar he was, and was irritated that I was not going to get that opportunity. I didn't like her decision but respected her right to make it, because Nichols was her case, and it was ultimately her call. As we were finishing up, Investigator Cindy Williamson walked up and stood next to me in the doorway. She worked with Gayle, and the two women were very close friends. I moved aside to let Cindy into Gayle's office and glanced to my left at the clock on the wall at the end of the hallway. I purposely stood in the doorway so I could watch the time. I needed to talk to

Gayle before the trial started, but I also had to appear before a different judge on another case that morning at 9 A.M. It was 9 A.M.

I turned back toward Gayle and Cindy and continued. "By the way, it seems we've convinced Nichols that we're going to win." Both of them looked at me and wondered why I was so sure. "On Wednesday, when court had just recessed for lunch, for some reason Nichols was sitting alone, and I was sitting at counsel table. He walked over to me and made the comment that we were doing a much better job this time around. I pointed to the transcript from the first trial and said, 'We know what everybody is going to say.' Then, this morning I was on the elevator and Sergeant White got on at the second floor. Just as I was getting off he said, 'Nichols knows he's going down this time.' The doors closed before I had a chance to ask him why he thought so. Nichols must have said something to trigger Sergeant White to make that comment."

Cindy shook her head in disgust. I suspected it was because of the reference to the first trial. She was appalled by the way Nichols lied, and manipulated his way to a hung jury in that trial. Having worked with Gayle for several years, she knew what was in store for him later in the morning. She didn't want to miss his testimony and the opportunity to watch him squirm during cross-examination. I glanced back at the clock on the wall. It was 9:01 A.M. I had to leave Gayle's office at that moment in order to get to the other judge's courtroom on time. I still needed to stop by my office and grab the files for the other judge's hearing. If that judge followed his usual pattern, he would not be on the bench until 9:10 or 9:15, which meant that I would not officially be late until 9:20. As I started to walk away from Gayle's door, a page came over the public announcement system in the office.

"All investigators report to the third floor. All investigators to the third floor." The announcement didn't startle me because there were a variety of reasons D.A. Investigators found themselves summoned to respond to various requests. Most of the time, they were more annoying than dangerous. I grabbed the files I needed from the corner of my desk, and headed toward the elevator.

Several investigators dispersed throughout the seventh floor, gathered in a group, and were moving toward the front of the office and the elevators. Cindy and three or four other investigators walked toward the elevator with me. Somebody mentioned that a deputy had been shot outside. Even that comment didn't alarm me. On some level, my lack of concern is a sad commentary on how being a criminal lawyer insidiously changes your perspective on life. One day you realize that you have become numb to tragic events that shock the conscience of most people. Violence and death are common occurrences in my world and over time, they simply lose their shock value. For example, after hearing about the shooting, people continued moving through their day not disturbed by the violence, but rather, irritated by the interruption it caused. At the time, I thought some mal-adjusted inmate had grabbed a deputy's gun but assumed that everything was under control. I remained focused on what I needed to do for the other judge and later that morning in the Nichols trial.

Cindy and her group stopped and waited for the elevator to arrive. I passed by Cindy, and said, "See you upstairs in a minute." I only needed to go up one flight of stairs, and it would be faster for me to walk than to wait on the elevator. When I passed through the door that leads to the stairs, I checked my watch one last time. I was confident I could get to the other courtroom, make my announcements, and get back to Judge Barnes' courtroom by 9:30 A.M.

As I quickly climbed the stairs, several thoughts were tumbling around in my mind. I wondered what deputy had been shot. For some reason, my thoughts turned to the arrogant grin Nichols wore during the first trial. I couldn't wait to see his lies uncovered and how he would react to being exposed. I opened the door to the eighth floor, and there was absolute bedlam. Almost simultaneously, things started to move in slow motion. Two deputies were standing in the middle of the hallway. I knew they were not assigned to the Nichols case, so their presence in the hallway seemed peculiar. I said to myself, "Why are they standing outside of Judge Barnes' chamber door?" One of the deputies commanded, "Clear the floor!" She didn't scream but spoke with the authority of someone in charge. Her order startled me but I wanted to see what was going on. Ignoring her for the moment, I slowly moved away from the stairwell door, out further into the courtyard, and scanned the area around me. To my left I could see the door to Judge Barnes' chambers. In front of me was the hallway that led to an exit from the building. Off to my right was the glass walkway that leads to the New Courthouse. Other than the number of people scurrying around, nothing about the area indicated any problem. However, there was a feeling of urgency that covered the area like a dark storm cloud. Cautiously, as though afraid to interrupt, I hesitantly asked one of the deputies what was going on. When he turned toward me with a bewildered look on his face, it was clear he had absolutely no idea. He replied, "I don't know, Ash. I don't know." By now, it was 9:03 A.M.

IN THE LINE OF DUTY

Time: 9:00 A.M.

ANYONE who knew Sergeant Hoyt Keith Teasley, a 17-year veteran of the Sheriff's Department, knew he took his duty to "Serve and Protect" seriously. He also held those that worked for him to the same high standard. Teasley would routinely challenge other Sheriff's Department employees about their knowledge of department policies and procedures. His tone was never condescending or disrespectful, and as a result, people admired and respected him as a leader. He often expressed his concern that if something were to happen at the Courthouse, few would know how to react. Ironically, his concern was prophetic.

Two weeks before March 11th, Teasley challenged Sergeant Starks about the interpretation of a particular department policy. Starks believed that if deputies were on their way to work, they should be in uniform. The theory being that if they were killed before arriving, the death would be considered in the line of duty. Teasley disagreed and stated that the deputy would actually have to be working for the death to be considered in the line of duty.

The two men agreed that Teasley would investigate the policy, and they would settle the friendly dispute later.

After clocking in at 9 A.M. that Friday morning, Teasley walked into the roll-call area on the ninth floor of the New Courthouse to report for duty. Starks, seated in a nearby area, noticed him and said hello. As Teasley replied to Starks, he heard a Code Yellow alarm from inside the Central Control room. He threw his lunch on the nearest table and took off running to respond to the call for help. Starks jumped up from his seat to follow but dropped his hat on the floor. Starks yelled, "Sergeant Teasley, hold the elevator!" Teasley either did not hear him or chose not to wait. In the fraction of time that it took Starks to bend down and pick up his hat, he missed getting onto the elevator with Teasley. As a result, Starks caught the next elevator and was seconds behind Teasley in responding to the alarm.

On the elevator ride down to the eighth floor, Starks heard Sergeant Grantley White yell over the radio that the Judge had been shot. Starks immediately recognized that unlike previous alarms, he and Teasley were responding to a real emergency. When the doors to the elevator opened, Starks took off running at top speed. He saw Teasley running down the hallway about 15 or 20 feet in front of him with his radio in his hand. Starks assumed that Teasley heard the distress call over his radio as a shooting, and was prepared to respond accordingly. As a result, he never called out to Teasley and assumed that they would react to the situation as trained.

When Starks made it to the glass walkway, he saw Teasley at the end of the walkway pass through the doors into the Old Courthouse, and bear to the right. When he saw Teasley run to the right, he assumed Teasley would enter through Judge Barnes' private chamber doors and cover the rear of the courtroom. Starks' training dictated that he cover the front of the courtroom. Unbeknownst to Starks, when Teasley passed through the doors at the end of the glass walkway he observed an unidentified black man run toward a secure exit doorway, which led to the street. Teasley gave chase to the unidentified black male and followed him down eight flights of stairs. When Sergeant Starks passed through the same doors at the end of the glass walkway, he went to the left to secure the front of the courtroom. When he entered the courtroom, he could still smell and see gun smoke. One woman, covered in blood, stood near the court reporter stand. She was shaking and screaming, but seemingly unable to move.

From the smell in the room, Starks knew the shooter was probably gone, but he remained cautious. With his side arm drawn, he walked over to the Judge's bench. His large black leather chair was twisted to the left, and his body lay in a pool of his own blood. When Starks looked down at him, he knew immediately that the man he had known and respected for 14 years was dead. Though he had fallen on his left side after being shot, the right side of his head faced the ceiling and exposed the exit wound from the bullet that killed him. Blood was everywhere. It covered the top of the bench, splattered the sides, and soaked into the carpet where his lifeless body had fallen. Starks could tell that the Judge suffered one fatal shot to the back of the head.

He turned to the woman screaming and yelled, "Which way did they go? Which way did they go?" Traumatized by witnessing the execution of her Judge, and horrified that the lifeless body of her Court Reporter fell onto her, Lynette Davis could not answer. Starks realized she would be of no help, so he turned and ran out of the main doors. What he had no way of knowing was that at the same time he ran out of the doors to the courtroom, other deputies were securing Judge Barnes' chambers and rescuing the hostages.

Meanwhile, Starks ran past the elevators in the lobby, and down the first set of stairs he came upon. When he reached the main floor of the Old Courthouse and swung the door open, nine or ten deputies faced him with their weapons drawn. He bolted past them and outside to the top of the steps of the Old Courthouse. Panic-stricken and alarmed by the sight of his gun, people ran for cover. All the while, Starks frantically searched the scattering crowd for the unidentified shooter. With no clear picture of what the shooter looked like, he noticed commotion near the Underground parking deck and quickly decided his shooter was the cause.

Starks would later learn that Teasley chased Brian Nichols down eight flights of stairs. With no other activity in the enclosed area, each man would have heard the other's footsteps echo off the walls of the stairwell. Teasley may have assumed he was chasing down an escaped prisoner, but he certainly was unaware the man was armed and only moments before had murdered two people in cold blood.

Nichols, more determined than before to evade capture, ran through the exit door and into the street. Aware that Sergeant Teasley was following closely behind him, Nichols waited for him to open the same door through which he had just come. Half way across Martin Luther King, Jr. Boulevard, Nichols heard the door open. He spun around in the middle of the street and fired several shots.

Sergeant Teasley, just ten days shy of his 44th birthday, did not have his weapon drawn. Instead, he only had his radio in his hand. When he heard the gun explode, he instinctively raised his right hand to shield himself and the first bullet struck him in that hand. As he fell to the ground, Nichols fired several more shots, at least one of which struck Teasley in the chest. Nichols turned and ran as Teasley fell to the ground. Lying on the cold concrete bleeding, he had become Nichols' ninth victim and fourth shooting victim in less than five minutes.

Police cars and deputies running on foot suddenly swarmed the scene looking for the shooter but instead found one of their own lying on the ground in a pool of blood. They knew Teasley needed medical care immediately, and did not want to wait for the ambulance to arrive. At first, they tried to load him into the back of a patrol car, then into the front, but he was too large to fit in either. They finally had to lay him back on the ground and allow the paramedics who arrived on the scene to take over. Sergeant Teasley would eventually make it to Grady Memorial Hospital by ambulance.

Only minutes from the Courthouse, Grady Hospital is the largest and most active trauma unit in the state of Georgia. For the doctors and staff of Grady, located within walking distance to downtown Atlanta, moving at a fast pace is part of the job. Saving lives in spite of chaos for them is normal, but even they were surprised by the crushing wave of people littering the hallways and the courtyard area of the hospital following the shootings. Several of the victims from the initial minutes of Nichols' rampage were transported to Grady Hospital for care. Relatives and friends of the victims flooded the facility praying their loved ones were alive. Police officers, listening over radios around the city and watching news coverage of the events, descended upon the Courthouse area and the hospital wanting to help in any way.

At work at the post office, Deborah Teasley thought about her husband when she learned of the shootings and even called his cell phone. When he did not answer, she assumed he was busy and thought of all the reasons he could not have been the injured deputy mentioned on the news. She thought to herself, Hoyt was not on duty yet, and probably was dropping their daughter off at school. Hoyt was also a supervisor and he did not work in the courtrooms. It couldn't be him they were talking about. She made a mental note to call him again later, and told her co-workers to let her know immediately if he called. Not long afterwards, she received a call she will never forget. The caller on the other end told her she needed to get to Grady Hospital because her husband was injured.

As she walked the crowded halls looking for her husband, she was taken aback by the number of people crying and leaning against walls for support. Officers in uniforms, nurses, and civilians comforted each other and sobbed, oblivious to those staring at them. The moment she rounded the corner of the room the woman at the nurses' station directed her to, she saw her mother-in-law. When she looked into her grief-stricken eyes, she knew her husband was gone. She never got the chance to say goodbye to Hoyt, her high school sweetheart and loving father to their two daughters.

Sergeant Hoyt Keith Teasley never got the chance to settle his friendly dispute with Sergeant Starks concerning the meaning of that department policy. Instead, his death serves as a concrete and unequivocal example of "killed in the line of duty."

• • •

Time: 9:01 A.M.

Friday March 11th started out like most for Lieutenant Robert Smith in the female inmate holding area. Immune to the hectic air of the inmate holding cells, he listened closely instead to chatter coming across his radio. Smith could hear Central Control trying to raise a radio response from Unit 1358. That Unit, assigned to Sergeant Grantley White, did not respond to the request, and Smith heard Central Control issue a Code Yellow. Smith continued to mill around the room with one ear listening to conversations amongst the deputies around him and the other tuned in to his radio. Moments later, Sergeant White's voice pierced the radio waves, and yelled for anyone listening to help. Smith bolted from the room and down the hall toward the elevators that led to the eighth floor. In mid stride, Smith heard White scream over the radio, "He's shot the Judge!"

Smith and several other deputies from the detention area packed the elevator used for transporting inmates from the holding cells to the courtrooms above. By now, they all knew that someone bold enough to shoot a Judge in a Courthouse was on the loose in the building. Nothing in his or any other deputy's training had prepared them for this moment. Nevertheless, each was determined to bring calm to an out-of-control situation. If only everyone responsible for Courthouse security had carried out their daily duties with the same fervor, perhaps March 11th would not now be infamous in the archives of Fulton County history. Were it not for matters of happenstance, coincidence, and incompetence, that day could just as easily be remembered as the day a rape defendant's verdict was handed down by a jury of his peers.

Deputies responded to Grantley White's plea for help and descended upon Judge Barnes' chambers. The smell of gunpowder greeted them as soon as they opened the door. They drew their weapons and systematically moved through the doors, looking for the shooter. One team of deputies first secured the chamber area. As they moved cautiously down the hallway checking the offices on either side, Deputy Harold Moore announced, "Is anyone here? Fulton County Deputies, show yourself now!" Somewhere off in the distance he heard a faint voice say, "We're here. We're in here." Deputy Moore ordered, "Identify yourself and your radio number!" A shaken male voice responded to the command. With remorse and anger heavier than his shoulders could bear, Sergeant White flatly responded, "Unit 1358. 1358." Distraught and defeated, Sergeant White emerged from Judge Barnes' inner office, followed by the other hostages.

Deputy Moore, one of the first deputies who secured the

chambers, holstered his side arm, removed his handcuff keys from his belt, and began to free the hostages. He then radioed to Central Control that the suspect was Brian Nichols and gave his physical description. The mentioning of his name caused Susan Christy to start thinking about her friends that would have had contact with Nichols. Suddenly, Deputy Cynthia Hall came to mind. Repeatedly, she screamed, "Where's Cynthia? Where's Cynthia?" Deputy Moore realized she was not accounted for and fled the room in search of his missing comrade.

DISCOVERIES

PART IV

An Uneasy Feeling

Time: 9:03 A.M.
"I knew something was terribly wrong."

I WAS standing in the middle of the floor outside the private entrance to Judge Barnes' chambers and was overwhelmed by the flurry of activity in the area. Deputies seemed to pour out of every doorway, crack, and crevice, moving quickly but never acknowledging my presence. Suddenly, I noticed an elderly black man sitting on one of the wooden benches with a look of disbelief on his face. I wondered whether he was one of the jurors from Nichols' case and simultaneously realized that it was. Then I thought, "Why is he sitting there by himself?"

My attention shifted to the reverberating cries of pain that seemed to bounce from one wall to the next in rapid-fire succession. I turned away from the juror and toward Judge Barnes' private entrance and saw two women hugging each other. I recognized the woman facing me as Susan Christy, Judge Barnes' calendar clerk. With her back to me, I did not recognize the other woman but could tell she was inconsolable. Both of them were crying uncontrollably. I thought they were crying because they knew the deputy who had been shot outside. I could not figure out, however, which deputy they were crying about. I knew it could not have been Deputy White because I had seen him only moments earlier on the elevator.

Before I could go over to Susan, the same Sergeant repeated her command to me. "I said get off the floor!" She continued to stare at me while she spoke into the radio attached to her shoulder. "Check the holding cell for Deputy Hall! She's not here! Check the holding cell! Check the holding cell!" The space between us was interrupted momentarily by Deputy Moore sprinting past me towards the New Courthouse. Uncertain of exactly what was happening, I knew I needed to leave the eighth floor. At the time, I had no idea Brian Nichols was the cause of the chaos around me. I turned to retreat through the stairwell doors I had come through moments before, and was almost trampled by deputies responding to unmasked distress calls coming over their radios. I eventually made it to the District Attorney offices on the seventh floor, still unsure of what had happened, and completely unaware of what was yet to come.

Delivering the Truth

Time 9:04 A.M.

RUNNING across the glass walkway in search of missing Deputy Hall, Deputy Harold Moore encountered Deputy Dorothy Abner. He knew she would have keys to the holding cells, and told her to follow him. Panting in between words, he tried to bring her up to speed as they ran. "We can't find Hall! We think he may have left her in a holding cell!" The two deputies ran directly to the secret door in the courtroom, which leads to the holding cells. Cautiously opening the door, he told her, "They also don't know where this Nichols guy is! Check the inmate elevator to see if he's in there!"

Both drew their weapons and Moore pushed the button for the inmate elevator door to open. After clearing that area, the next door Moore opened was to the cell that held Deputy Hall. She was struggling to get up and Moore gently touched her shoulder telling her to relax because help was on the way. Deputy Abner moved away. She and Hall were friends and neighbors, and seeing her so badly injured was difficult. She instead focused her attention on being ready to respond if Nichols reappeared.

With her weapon drawn, Deputy Abner stood watch at the door between the courtroom and the holding cells.

Within minutes, another Fulton County Deputy, Lieutenant Robert Smith, arrived on the scene and the shocking sight stopped him in his tracks at the door. Smears and splatters of blood covered the walls of the small holding cell. The strong foul smell was unlike anything Smith had ever encountered. It was as though death was in the room, and its next conquest lay on the floor before him. He knelt beside her and said, "Miss Hall? Do you hear me?"

Struggling to speak or even move, Deputy Hall could only let out a weak moan. Lieutenant Smith, determined not to lose her, talked to her and reassured her things would be okay. "Okay, stay with me now. Help is on the way." Lieutenant Smith remained by her side as the EMT workers tried to stabilize her condition before moving her to an ambulance. Deputy Abner, still standing guard at the door, could hear over her radio that Nichols had been spotted in the parking garage across the street, and all were certain that he was no longer in the Courthouse. She holstered her weapon and stood quietly against the door. Watching them bandage Deputy Hall's head while placing an oxygen mask over her mouth, she waited for the Lieutenant to give her further instructions. He said, "I'm going down with her. You two stay here and make sure that nobody disturbs this scene." With that, Lieutenant Smith turned and trotted alongside the gurney rushing Deputy Hall to the ambulance. Once on the first floor, Lieutenant Smith ignored the mobs of deputies and people staring at them. His sole focus was making sure that no one got in the way of the people trying to help one of his own. Once she was loaded in the ambulance and they sped off, he finally seemed to notice all the activity around him. He saw a woman in a uniform he did not recognize talking into a radio. She spoke in codes unfamiliar to him and then said, "Another deputy's coming in."

Lieutenant Smith moved closer to the woman and asked the name of the other deputy. Anxiously, the woman turned to him and said, "It's Deputy Teasley. He's been shot!" Smith felt numb. He thought to himself, "How could all of this happen?" Slowly, he turned and walked back inside the Courthouse. He needed to clear the holding cell of any emergency equipment left there. As he got off the elevator on the eighth floor, a young detention officer he did not know approached him and asked, "Are you Smitty?" Annoyed by answering unnecessary questions he flatly responded, "Yeah."

"Someone's looking for you over there." Reluctantly, he turned and followed the young woman to a jury deliberating room. As soon as he rounded the corner, he immediately saw who wanted him. Only her side profile was facing him, but they had been friends and worked together in the Courthouse long enough for him to recognize her silhouette instantly. She worked for Judge Mather as a judicial assistant and was in the building when the shootings occurred. The young officer who led him to the room moved to the side and the woman whose head was down, turned to face her friend of many years. As if willing an answer different than the one she knew would come, she said, "I've known you a long time. Tell me what's going on." At that moment, he knew no one had told her what happened to her husband of ten years. He knew there would be no more Friday nights together at their favorite Mexican restaurant. Their Friday night ritual was so predictable, police officers routinely dropped by during their meal to have the Judge sign a warrant or merely share a moment of his time. Dread flooded his entire body as the seconds slowly passed, and he imagined the ways in which her life would never be the same. He came to grips with the fact that he would have to deliver the horrible news, and as a result, his life also would never be the same. He asked her, "What have you been told?"

"That there's been a shooting. Is Rowland okay?" Her eyes

begged for him to say yes. Lieutenant Smith looked away from her and at the others in the room. There were some he recognized by face from seeing them around the Courthouse Complex and others whose names he knew. He saw a friend of hers who worked with her for many years. He did not want to deliver such life-altering news in front of a room full of strangers. He walked over and gently grabbed her by the elbow and said, "Follow me." He motioned for the friend to come along as well, because he knew she would need as much support as possible. Once away from the others, he quietly said, "He's dead." Claudia Barnes collapsed against Lieutenant Smith's chest and sobbed.

COVERING HIS TRACKS

Time: 9:05 A.M.

AFTER firing several shots at Sergeant Teasley and killing him, Nichols ran onto Martin Luther King, Jr. Boulevard. He knew he did not have much time to complete his escape from the area, as Sheriff's Deputies were certain to have discovered the bodies in the courtroom and were bound to discover Teasley at any moment. Without hesitation, he faced oncoming traffic brandishing one of the two county-issued handguns he confiscated from the defeated deputies and tried to stop any car that passed. Drivers swerved to avoid hitting him as their cars barreled toward him. He ignored the sounds of screeching brakes and honking horns and continued across the busy street toward the Underground parking garage.

Nichols ran up to a stopped car sitting at the entrance to the garage. As the second car in line waiting to take a ticket from the automated parking attendant, Atlanta Deputy Solicitor Duane Cooper sat behind the wheel of his 2001 Mazda Tribute. Cooper rolled down his window and leaned over to pick up his brief case. When he looked back, Nichols was standing at his window with a gun aimed at his left temple. His calm demeanor alarmed Cooper as much as the gun pointed toward him. "Put it in park and get out." Nichols did not raise his voice or seem in a hurry. Cooper knew instantly that the armed man would kill him if he put up any resistance. Without any further conversation, Cooper opened the door to his SUV and watched in stunned silence as Nichols screeched backwards out of the entrance and raced toward Peachtree Street. As Nichols took off, Cooper ran to the skid marks left in the street and stood in shock as his SUV disappeared, turning right at the top of the hill. Only then did he notice the crowd gathering around Sergeant Teasley. A police car screeched to a stop between Cooper and the crowd gathered around the dying officer. Cooper heard someone scream, "Which way did he go? Which way did he go?" followed by more squealing tires and blazing sirens. Meanwhile, aware that police would quickly determine the make, model, and license plate number for the stolen SUV, Nichols knew he needed to abandon it.

Tow truck driver Deronta Franklin sat in his rig on Wall Street around the corner from the Courthouse. With the front of his truck facing Peachtree Street and a parking garage immediately to his right, he waited for his next call from dispatch. Deronta noticed a car speed up Peachtree Street, make a quick right turn onto Wall Street, and an even quicker left turn in front of him into the parking garage. He could not see the driver very well, nor could he see that the driver took a ticket from the meter box and illegally parked the SUV behind another vehicle, blocking it from leaving its parking space. He did see, however, that moments after the SUV pulled into the garage, a trail of police cars with sirens and lights on full tilt raced past Wall Street.

Seconds later, Nichols walked from the garage and over to Deronta. As he got closer to the truck, Deronta noticed that his shirt was covered in blood, and as soon as the sight registered in his brain, Nichols flashed a gun and said, "Let me have it." Deronta did not care enough about the truck to die being a hero. He threw his hands in the air and said, "You can have the truck."

Nichols got into the passenger side of the truck and slid over to the driver's side. Leaving Deronta standing in the street, Nichols drove forward, waited for a few cars to pass, and then turned right onto Peachtree Street. As he disappeared from sight, Deronta ran across the street to the Underground Mall looking for the nearest police officer. It was 9:07 A.M.

Meanwhile, Nichols drove through three lights until he came to Luckie Street. He turned left onto Luckie, made another quick left onto Cone Street, and entered another parking garage. At about the same time, Almeta Kilgo, a 37-year-old computer programmer for The Atlanta Journal-Constitution newspaper, maneuvered her 2004 Mercury Sable into her usual parking space. When she backed into her parking space, she noticed a tow truck parked in the space directly across from her. She wondered if the driver was going to give her a ticket or tow someone's car. Almeta saw him jump out of the tow truck as she opened her car door. Before she knew it, Nichols put a gun to her head and told her to move over. Almeta moved over to the passenger side of her sedan and Nichols started the engine. After he drove the car down several levels below where she originally parked, he ordered her to get into the trunk. She knew if she did, he certainly would kill her. At that moment, Almeta decided she was not going to die in the trunk of her car. Nichols opened the driver's side door and ordered her to open the passenger's side. Seizing the opportunity to save her life, Almeta ran away screaming for help but tripped and fell. Nichols jumped out of the car and raced over to her. As she lay on her back screaming, Nichols pointed a gun in her face. Presumably calculating in his mind whether or not to shoot her, he ultimately decided not to kill her. Instead, he ran back to her car and sped off. It was 9:14 A.M.

His next stop was a parking garage at 250 Spring Street. Small-business owner Sung Chung was getting out of his green Isuzu Trooper when Nichols appeared beside him. He told Chung to move over to the passenger seat. Chung looked from the gun in his hand to the blood on his shirt and complied. Nichols told the man he wanted all of the money he had on him. By this time, he was maneuvering Chung's Trooper through the parking deck trying to get back to the street. When Chung replied he had no money on him, he noticed Nichols no longer had the gun in his hand. Nichols was trying to steer the truck while he took off his blood-soaked shirt. Chung seized the opportunity to escape and jumped from the moving car and took off running. Nichols never slowed down. It was 9:16 A.M.

Turning back onto Spring Street, his next destination was the Centennial Parking garage at 130 Marietta Street. Undoubtedly to his surprise, a motorcycled police officer and two squad cars suddenly appeared in the rearview mirror. Only a few blocks from the Courthouse, he turned into another parking garage smashing through the gate. The two parking attendants, startled by the sound of the gate crashing and tires squealing, backed away from the flying debris. Seconds later the police arrived at the entrance and yelled, "Which way did he go?" One of the attendants, Frank Holston, tried in vain to tell the officers that Nichols had gone into the parking garage, but instead of following him, they should block the only two exits. One exit was for vehicle traffic. The other exit to the left of the attendant booth was for foot traffic. Instead of listening to Holston and blocking the exits, all three units sped into the garage.

At the same time, several levels above, Atlanta Journal-Constitution newspaper book reviewer Don O'Briant was parking his 1997 four-door green Honda Accord. Nichols parked the stolen SUV Trooper in a handicapped space next to O'Briant's car and asked the older man for directions to Lennox Square. O'Briant noticed that Nichols did not have on a shirt under his suit jacket, but assumed the stranger was in town for the NCAA Men's Basketball tournament and was attempting to make a fashion statement. Suddenly, Nichols ordered the reporter to give him the keys to his car. O'Briant resisted and Nichols responded by calmly repeating the command. As an extra measure of comfort to ensure his compliance, Nichols shoved the gun toward him and said, "Give me the keys or I'll kill you." After O'Briant handed over the keys, Nichols ordered him into the trunk. O'Briant looked into the vacant eyes of the tall muscular man in front of him and knew if he did, death certainly would be his fate. Instead, he turned to run. But this time, Nichols did not let another victim simply escape. He no doubt realized the reason the police suddenly appeared on his tail after he so cleverly disposed of four different stolen vehicles in under ten minutes was because he left all of the victims standing unharmed. He did not need to kill O'Briant, only slow him down. He mercilessly pistol-whipped the 62-year-old reporter before stealing his car and speeding away. It was 9:20 A.M.

Hearing police sirens bouncing off the walls of the garage, Nichols drove the Honda down one level below where he had taken it and altered his plan to escape by car. Wearing a suit jacket, no shirt, and with two guns concealed in his pants, Nichols entered the closest stairwell. With his hands in his pockets, and the sides of his jacket tucked into the folds of his arms, Nichols brazenly bared his chest as he casually strolled down the stairs to the street exit. Parking attendant Frank Holsten and his co-worker saw Nichols emerge from the stairs and walk down Spring Street toward the CNN news building. They noticed Nichols glance at the stairwell behind him after every few steps to see if anyone discovered that he was now on foot. To them, he never appeared to be in a hurry or worried.

Nichols eventually boarded a MARTA train headed for Buckhead, one of the busiest areas of the city. Ironically, MARTA police, like the Sheriff's Department and Atlanta Police before them, also miscalculated Nichols' next move. That could be the only explanation why authorities pulled MARTA police from train stations nearby and sent them to the Courthouse already inundated with law enforcement officers. Another critical law

enforcement mistake was the failure to shut down MARTA bus
and train services. If only MARTA police had been left in place, or
if the Atlanta Police had blocked the stairwell of the last parking
garage, or if the Sheriff's Department had assigned more than
one deputy to escort Nichols to the holding cells in the first place,
terror for the four million citizens of Atlanta may have ended
before noon. Instead, Atlanta was a city under siege for another
24 hours.

Unspoken Pact

AS Sergeant Starks ran down an emergency exit stairwell in the Old Courthouse in search of a killer, Fulton County District Attorneys Matt Buzzelli and Tony Volkadov approached the front stairs of the same building. The two men who often car-pooled together, also worked in Judge Barnes' courtroom. As they started to walk up the steps of the Courthouse, a woman ran from the building toward them screaming, "He's got a gun! He's got a gun!"

Tony, a 15-year veteran of the Atlanta Police Department before attending law school and joining the Prosecutor's office, instinctively took cover behind one of the mammoth light fixtures that flank the front steps of the Courthouse. Without asking any questions, Matt followed suit. The two men felt as though they were in the middle of a Spanish bull-run as throngs of people rushed toward them.

Matt noticed deputies running down the sidewalk, weaving in and out of the crowd of people, headed toward the parking garage where he and Tony had exited seconds earlier. As more deputies appeared at the doors of the Courthouse blocking the entrance, the two men believed it safe to emerge from the sunken stairs behind the light fixture. They listened to the conversations of people around them in hopes of determining the cause of the commotion, but no one seemed to know. They would later learn that the armed man the unidentified woman screamed about was Sergeant Starks running toward the building exit looking for Judge Barnes' shooter.

Eventually, they climbed the massive curved stairs of the Old Courthouse and approached one of the deputies standing guard. Matt recognized one deputy by face but did not know his name. He spoke first, and asked the deputy, "Hey, what's going on?" The deputy, preoccupied with searching the crowd for an armed gunman without the benefit of a physical description of the person he was looking for, responded without ever taking his eyes off the crowd. "Judge Barnes was shot in the head, and he's not going to make it." Both men stared at the deputy as if he spoke to them in a foreign language. They faced each other searching for some sign that each had heard the deputy correctly. After what seemed like an eternity, but was less than a minute, the deputy told them they would have to clear the stairs. "The building is closed for now. Nobody in or out." Numb and in disbelief, they turned and walked down the steps. As word passed through the crowd gathered outside, people alternately expressed feelings of shock and fear. Pockets of people dotted the street and stood staring at the Old Courthouse. Tony and Matt overheard someone in the crowd mention Julie's name. Both men reeled from the news that she was dead as well. People were hugging one another, all the while astounded at the reality of a shooting inside the Courthouse. Some openly asked the question others merely thought, but everyone wanted to know, "How does someone get a gun in the building and kill a judge?"

Tony started picturing his Judge and shook his head in disbelief. For him Judge Barnes was the last person in the world that deserved to die in such a callous manner. Of all the judges he could think of, Judge Barnes was one of the few that always treated people fairly.

The first time Tony met Judge Barnes, he summoned Tony to his chambers and told his secretary to bring him a Polaroid camera. As a former police officer, Tony did not like to be photographed or fingerprinted. When the Judge requested the camera, he felt an irrational sense of anxiety about having his picture taken. The Judge noticed his discomfort but gave no reassuring words to alleviate his concerns. After the Judge took his picture, he pulled a large photo album from a credenza in his office and chuckled as Tony visibly relaxed. After asking him when his birthday was, Judge Barnes explained to Tony that every prosecutor and criminal defense attorney assigned to his courtroom was in that book. For the Judge, those people represented an extended family, and he treated them as such. At the time, Tony didn't realize that celebrating his birthday meant he was susceptible to the Judge's joking nature. Judge Barnes routinely celebrated birthdays by purchasing cakes, which read, "Happy Bar Mitzvah Mike," or some other unrelated wording scrawled across the icing. Tony often opted to bring his lunch and eat with the Judge and the rest of his staff in his chambers. He thought about how much the Judge enjoyed having people around his kitchen table breaking bread together. The Judge's annual Christmas party, a staple around the holiday season, suddenly came to mind.

News of the shootings was beginning to appear on local and national news stations. Consequently, every few minutes Matt's and Tony's cell phones' vibrations distracted them from their thoughts. Family and friends of both men, who knew they worked with Judge Barnes, called concerned for their safety. The conversations of each call were the same, so much so, they started each one with "I'm fine" instead of "Hello."

Standing near the entrance of the Old Courthouse and

unable to get into the building, they eventually walked around the corner to the entrance of the New Courthouse. Within minutes, Matt noticed two armed deputies escorting Susan Christy from the building to a waiting car. With her arms clutched across her chest, and a dark coat draped over her shoulders, she walked with her head hung low. She never looked up and was oblivious to the massive crowd gathered outside of the Courthouse. Matt nudged Tony, who had not yet noticed Susan, and the two called her name as they ran toward her. One of the deputies stepped in front of them and blocked them from getting closer to her. The sight of the two men whom she knew from working in the courtroom with Judge Barnes and Julie, instantly reminded her of the shootings. Crying hysterically, Susan pushed her way past the deputy and fell into the arms of her friends. She pleaded with the two of them to check on the Judge and Julie. "Make sure they're okay! Check on Julie and Judge Barnes! Make sure they're okay!" Both Tony and Matt held onto her, uncertain what to say.

The deputies finally pried her from Matt's arms and Tony instinctively loosened his grip. They ushered her into the waiting police car while Tony and Matt came to the realization that she had no idea their friends already were dead. Though neither of them discussed the decision, their instincts confirmed that that moment was not the time to deliver another crushing blow by telling her the truth. With tear-filled eyes, she reluctantly turned away and allowed the officers to close the car door. The two grief-stricken men stood curbside as the car sped away. They grieved the loss of their friends and for the pain those losses would cause others close to them. Tony thought about his last conversation with the Judge on the Tuesday before the shootings. He was considering applying for a job in a different county, and he discussed the possible move with his mentor and friend. Judge Barnes offered to call the man that would be his boss and recommend him for the position. Tony expressed his gratitude and thanked the Judge for his support. What Tony would not learn until several weeks after the shootings was that Judge Barnes in fact made the call, and his recommendation, in part, led to Tony being offered the job.

Standing in silence on the curb outside the New Courthouse other realities occurred to both men. They realized that more than any other time they spent together, that single moment, when they silently agreed not to tell Susan the harsh truth, formed a pact between them and inextricably linked the two friends together forever.

Beginning of the Tidal Wave

Time: 9:15 A.M.
"I'm still in the dark."

BACK inside the D.A.'s offices on the seventh floor, I was confused by the commotion all around me. With all the Investigators summoned to the third floor, away from our offices, I felt clueless. Normally, Tracy Baker or Cindy Williamson were my sources of information, because they always had first-hand knowledge of what was going on in and around the building.

Slowly, people started to appear on our floor that ordinarily were not there, and their presence felt eerily out of place. As I walked through one of the hallways of our offices, I came upon one person who was talking about a deputy shot outside on the street. In another hallway, I heard a different person saying a judge had been shot. As people listened to the stories, they would pass the new information to another group of people eagerly awaiting word of the unfolding events. Neither District Attorney Paul Howard, nor anyone in his command, ever made any official announcement, and as a result, those word of mouth communications were crucial. I suddenly realized I didn't know where Suparna was or whether she was in the building.

• • •

Time: 9:15 A.M.
"I placed my 1ˢᵗ call to Suparna."

As I stood in the doorway of my office, I pulled my cell phone from my pocket, and pressed "pound 1," which instantly dialed Suparna. I could hear the line ringing in my Bluetooth earpiece, so I closed the phone and put it back into my pocket, "Hey, where are you?"

"I'm on my way to the jail. Why?"

"There's been a shooting down here."

"What?"

"Yeah, a deputy and a judge. Don't come down here. The streets are blocked off. It's just crazy. Go back home and I'll call you later." I honestly don't remember if I even let her respond before I ended the call. My sixth sense that something was drastically awry was kicking into gear, and I went back into the hallway searching for more information.

In the meantime, Suparna hung up the phone and wondered to herself, "What judge and what deputy?" Luckily for her, traffic was moving slower than usual on GA Route 400. As a result, she had not passed the exit nearest their home and could get off the expressway without having to fight too much traffic. She zipped through the streets of Buckhead, winding her way past stores with workers arriving for the day and through busy residential neighborhoods, until she entered the Brookhaven area they called home. Not particularly concerned about the news Ash had delivered moments before, she turned onto her street and thought of her children greeting her at the door. They were home from school and would be thrilled to see she had taken the day off to be with them.

GATHERING EVIDENCE

Time: 9:15 A.M.

AROUND the same time Ash entered the tidal wave of activity in the D.A.'s offices, fate was about to pull Al Dixon into the outbreak of confusion as well. After 27 years with the Fulton County District Attorney's Office, Dixon previously scheduled a much needed vacation day for March 11th. It was approximately 9:15 A.M. and standing at his kitchen counter in front of the coffeemaker, Dixon heard his cell phone ring in the other room. With its distinctive ring tone, he instantly recognized the beckoning of the office. Set to retire on April 10th, for a split second he thought to himself, "Ron's the D.A. on call, and whatever it is he can handle it." Yet, he started walking toward the ringing cell phone.

Most of his years with the office were spent in the Homicide Unit, the last several as Chief of the unit, and they had taken their toll. Dixon walked more than his fair share of murder scenes roped off with yellow crime tape, and watched his reflection in the mirror slowly age as both criminals and victims seemed to get younger and younger. Like people addicted to smoking who found it difficult to quit, Dixon was addicted to the rush of solving crimes and punishing those guilty. Walking away cold turkey was almost impossible, but it was time for him to start the slow walk toward retirement. Moving to a District Attorney's Office in an outer-lying county with a lower crime rate and a correspondingly less demanding trial schedule would help him along the journey.

Never one to shun his responsibilities, Dixon answered the call. The voice on the other end struggled to remain calm and announced, "Mr. Dixon there's been a shooting inside the Courthouse." Dixon's mindset and demeanor immediately shifted into automatic pilot and he replied, "I'm on my way." Two parallel streams of thought simultaneously raced through his mind as he grabbed his keys and coat. He first thought of the need to protect the crime scene. With all of the people who pass through the Courthouse on a daily basis, the crime scene easily could be contaminated. Protecting it was paramount because whoever was bold enough to fire a gun inside a Courthouse needed to be brought to justice. He thought about how he found it useful to walk through crime scenes. As a result, he routinely arrived at the scene of a crime while the police were still processing the scene for evidence and canvassing the area for witnesses. Doing so made it easier for him to visualize how crimes occurred. This in turn made his arguments to jurors more persuasive later. He could trust Ron to recognize the importance of the courtroom as a crime scene and ensure it was not contaminated. His second train of thought shifted to the victims. "Who were they? Were they witnesses set to testify at a trial? Where were the deputies when the shooting happened?" The torrent of questions flowing through his mind was endless. The secretary from the office that phoned had very little information and left him with more questions than answers.

Dixon lived only 15 minutes from the Courthouse, and it would not take him long to get there. As he sped through residential tree-lined streets and onto congested major thoroughfares, he started thinking of all of his friends that worked in the Courthouse. He began listing in his mind any D.A.'s that reported to him who might be in trial and the courtrooms to which they were assigned. One friend in particular registered on top of his list. He was a Superior Court Judge, and the two men had been good friends and neighbors for over 18 years. Dixon knew that his friend was due to be in session conducting the re-trial of a rape suspect. He suddenly felt the need to get more information about the shootings. He phoned his secretary only to learn she had no new information. As he drove down the entrance ramp onto Interstate 85, he decided to phone another friend of his from the Atlanta police department. For many who knew him during his days as a police officer, he was still "Dix," and his calls never went unanswered.

"Hey, what's going on over at the Courthouse?"

"I'm on my way there. Best info I've got right now – two dead in the building and at least one sheriff outside."

"Do we know who's dead inside?"

"A Judge and somebody else. Maybe somebody on his staff. I'm not sure."

Already on edge from the news of a shooting inside the Courthouse, Dixon scrutinized every word of the conversation that followed. Before he asked his next question, he suspected he knew the answer, but continued hoping his instinct was wrong.

"Who's the judge?"

"Rowland Barnes. Did you know him?"

With words caught in his throat, Dixon glanced upward, noticed the exit sign for Fulton Street, and mechanically steered his car off the highway. He ignored the question and continued searching for answers. "Do we know who did this?"

"I don't have much info on that yet, but it looks like it was an escaped prisoner."

"A prisoner? Huh. Well, thanks for the update."

"Don't mention it."

Dixon closed his phone and slammed it into the seat

next to him. He pulled up to a red light and absent-mindedly looked around. Closing his eyes, he pounded his fist onto the steering wheel, and immediately caught himself. Barnes was a good friend of his and going to pieces was not going to help or change anything. As he got closer to the Courthouse, the swirl of activity was alarming. The streets were flooded with stopped traffic because officers closed the perimeter blocks surrounding the Courthouse. The only exceptions were police and emergency vehicles. Sirens blasted from every direction and flashing blue lights bounced off every nearby window. Dixon rolled down his window, flashed his Fulton County badge to one of the officers stopping traffic, then maneuvered his way through the maze of cars and shell-shocked people.

Chief Investigator Jim Strozer met Dixon near the glass revolving doors of the New Courthouse. The two golfing buddies acknowledged each other, then headed for the eighth floor of the Old Courthouse. Strozer, who is known as a man of few words, and even less patience, quickly brought Dixon up to speed. Dixon held up his hand and stopped the irritated Strozer in mid-sentence. "Is Judge Barnes gone?" Though he knew the answer before he asked the question, he held out hope that the police officer he talked to earlier was wrong. In times of crisis, it is not unusual for officers to get parts of a story incorrect. Maybe this was one of those times.

"I doubt he even knew what hit him." Strozer leveled his hard stare on Dixon, and the weight of his words rested on Dixon's shoulders like five-ton boulders. Dixon looked away and the two men simultaneously stepped onto the waiting elevator. "What do we know about who did this?"

"It was an escaped prisoner named Brian Nichols. That much we know. We're trying to nail down an accurate description, but his hostages. . ."

Interrupting Strozer's recitation Dixon said, "Hostages? What hostages?" Unfazed by the incredulous tone of Dixon's questions,

Strozer continued, "He took several people hostage in the Judge's suite beforehand. Some people on the Judge's staff, a lawyer and Grantley."

Dixon let out an exasperated huff, as if to say what will this guy do next and then quickly silenced the voice in his head. As of that moment, Nichols remained on the loose and based upon the bold crimes he had already committed, Dixon believed anything was possible. Strozer continued to bring Dixon up to speed. "The hostages are a bit shaken, and we're having a tough time getting a good description." The elevator stopped and the doors opened. The number of officers, sheriffs, and security detail present in the lobby area would have been unsettling to most people, but Dixon, in Homicide investigation mode, was unaffected. Though no individual voice or conversation was above a slight whisper, it seemed loud. It was certainly louder than the Judge would have tolerated outside his courtroom doors. As always, the Judge's "Quiet. Court in session." sign stood sentinel to the left of the doors to the courtroom. The difference this day was that the sign was used as the beginning of yellow crime scene tape that roped off the area.

Dixon lifted the badge hanging from his neck high enough for the officer guarding the door to read. The officer nodded his acceptance, and raised the yellow tape for Dixon to cross under and into one of the open doors.

When Dixon walked into the courtroom, D.A.'s Boyter and McCutchen were huddled together in the back of the room. He joined them and the two filled in information that Strozer left out. D.A. McCutchen spoke first.

"Deputy Teasley was also killed and Deputy Hall was shot in the face."

"Where was Deputy Teasley killed?"

"He was shot outside on the Martin Luther King side of the Courthouse, virtually in the street. There are people securing and processing that crime scene and the one for Deputy Hall."

"Where was she shot?"

Boyter broke into the conversation. "She was in the holding cell. He obviously took her out before coming over here."

Information needed to be relayed succinctly, and to that end, everyone was trying to remain detached from the events around them. In spite of that, this was no ordinary crime scene. These people were their friends. The person responsible for this carnage would pay, and no mistakes would be made in the investigation, particularly if Dixon had any say in the matter. The three lawyers turned away from each other and faced the well of the courtroom. Their politics varied as much as their years of job experience, but each had the same thought, "How could this happen inside the courtroom?"

Dixon called his boss on the telephone. As soon as Paul Howard answered the phone, Dixon could tell he already knew about the shootings. "I'm on my way back to the Courthouse right now." Howard wanted to know who were the District Attorneys trying the case. Dixon told him that it was Ash and Gayle.

"Where are they now?"

"I don't know but I think they're down on the seventh floor. I haven't seen or spoken with either of them." Dixon heard him move the phone away from his mouth and speak to someone else in the car with him. He presumed that Howard was talking to the head of his private security detail M.C. Cox. He assumed Howard was instructing Cox to get security for Ash and Gayle, but he did not focus on Howard's side conversation. Howard came back to the phone. "Do we have any other info?"

"Not right now. They are still processing the courtroom and there are at least two other crime scenes that we know of."

"Okay. I'll be on my cell."

Camera flashes seemed to click every few seconds, and people covered in sterile white outfits poured over every inch of the room. Their investigation would help in the prosecution that would inevitably come, but Dixon had to do his own walk-through of the scene. He had to see the crime from Nichols' viewpoint. He had to walk around the bodies of his friends. He could not help but think to himself, "If ever there were two people who deserved such a horrible fate, it would not have been these two."

One of the members of the crime scene investigation team asked aloud to anyone else on the team, "Do we know the caliber of the two guns used?" Everyone in the room turned in his direction and someone else spoke, "Not sure yet if he got county issues or not." The first man spoke again. "I got another slug over here." Another person with a camera walked over and took a picture of the bullet before carefully picking it up and sealing it in a clear plastic evidence bag. The team collecting evidence started to pack away their equipment. The Chief Forensic Investigator caught Dixon's attention and nodded his head, acknowledging that their business there was done. Dixon steeled himself and walked toward Barnes' bench. As he got closer, he noticed that both victims lay in the spot where they had fallen. He thought to himself, "They must have died instantly."

As he stood next to Rowland Barnes, Dixon reflected over the years and times the two men had shared. Like Dixon, Barnes started his career on a different path but came into his own on the bench. It was ironic that Dixon's time with Fulton County would end with him overseeing the prosecution of a defendant that executed his good friend. His mind flashed between vivid pictures of Rowland alive and well, and the lifeless, bloodied body lying at his feet. It was becoming more and more difficult for Dixon to remain objective and composed. His emotions started to overwhelm him. He could feel tears searing their way through his will power and turned away before he totally lost control. Moving away from Rowland's body, he saw Julie's lifeless body on the floor next to her chair. Clearly, she had turned in the direction of the shots fired at Rowland, and then tried to get away. She too, was shot in the back of the head. These were people he deeply cared about and pretending this was an ordinary crime scene was pointless. Angry, Dixon walked to the back of the courtroom. He watched as his friends were loaded into black body bags and individually lifted onto hospital gurneys. Seeing his friends carried away, Dixon's anger turned to fury. He knew that if the police ever caught Nichols, he would face the death penalty, but for Dixon, even that was not justice enough.

HEIGHTENED ANXIETY

Time: 9:30 A.M.
"I placed my 2nd call to Suparna."

WORD passed through the office that a member of the staff had a gun put to her head in the Underground parking deck across the street from the building. Reports were coming in of an unknown number of people being car-jacked in and around the parking garage. I overheard someone say that not only had a judge been shot but a court reporter as well. I walked over to the group of people talking and asked the name of the judge. Someone, though I don't remember who, said it was Judge Goger.

My first thought was that Brian Nichols was in the holding cells connected to Judge Goger's courtroom, but I instantly dismissed the thought from my mind. I couldn't allow myself to think he was behind this madness. The mere thought was too terrible to imagine. Standing in the hallway next to my office, I thought to myself, "Who in the hell is doing this?"

Growing more concerned as time went on, I called Suparna again. As soon as she answered, I said, "They think it was Goger.

They're also saying it was a court reporter. Do not come down here. Where are you now?"

"I just pulled up to the house. How are they?"

"We don't know yet." As I talked to her, I started aimlessly walking toward the receptionist area of the office.

"Where are you?" Suparna put her minivan in park and turned it off, but stayed behind the wheel.

"I'm in the office. I'll call you back." Once again, I just hung up the phone. I wasn't trying to be mean, but I wasn't concerned about being polite.

Suparna told me later, that she walked into the house, greeted the kids and was momentarily distracted by their enthusiasm to see her. At that time, neither of us was concerned our family was in any danger.

• • •

Uncertain when Ash would call again with more information, Suparna walked over to the coffee table in the family room and grabbed the television remote control. She put her son down and changed the channel from cartoons to a local news station. Both children immediately started to protest. The nanny intervened and quieted them with the promise of warm milk. The children quickly forgot about their mother's transgression and followed the Nanny to the refrigerator. Their focus returned to their mother when they heard the remote control crash to the table.

When Suparna tuned to WSB news, a picture of her Judge's face flashed across the screen followed by Julie Brandau's. On shaky legs, she stared at the television and tried to process what she was seeing. She could see the faces of her friends on the screen, but the reporter's words would not register in her mind. She had just seen Judge Barnes and Julie the previous afternoon. He smiled in her direction, while she and Julie talked briefly during a recess in the Nichols trial. Pulled from her thoughts by her daughter's light touch, Suparna turned the television back to cartoons. After bending down and reassuringly planting a kiss on her daughter's forehead, Suparna left the room. As she walked by the nanny standing at the kitchen sink she said, "Keep them out here." Once inside the office off the kitchen, she quietly closed the door behind her and rushed to the computer.

Stunned by the revelations on the news, she robotically typed keys on the computer, navigating her way to the CNN website. Desperate for more information, she stared at Judge Barnes' gruff smiling face on the screen before her. Staring back at the image on her computer screen, she struggled to understand the unimaginable.

A HUNCH BECOMES REALITY

Time: 9:30 A.M.

CROSS the street from the Old Courthouse is the
Fulton County Government Center, which houses
among other government offices, the main cafeteria
that serves the entire Courthouse Complex. After leaving their
weekly investigators' meeting, Tracy Baker and Mike Crawford
grabbed a table and sat down to their morning cup of java.
As the two men traded stories about their weekends, Tracy
remembered his uneasiness during the department meeting
when Cindy talked about the Defendant in her rape trial. He
waited for a pause in Mike's reverie about his weekend, and
contemplated whether he would mention his concern. Mike
paused, and seemingly on cue, they heard someone say there
had been a shooting on the eighth floor of the Old Courthouse.
Immediately, Tracy thought about Cindy and the Nichols trial.
He said, "I bet it's in the courtroom." He jumped from his chair
and looked across the courtyard and over to the front of the Old
Courthouse.

He pulled his cell phone from his pocket to call Cindy.
With no uniform method of communicating with each other,

most investigators took it upon themselves to keep the phone numbers of other investigators programmed into their personal cell phones. He and Mike ran from the Government Center to the street between the two buildings. The moment she answered, he knew his hunch from earlier in the morning was dreadfully correct. "What's going on? Are you okay?"

Even though Cindy was holding her cell phone in her hand, its sudden vibration signaling a call startled her. By that time, she knew there had been a shooting and that Judge Barnes and Julie were hurt. She had taken Lisa, the rape victim, and her mother Barbara to a secure area and waited for more information before deciding what to do next.

Turning away from the frightened mother and daughter, Cindy struggled to contain her emotions as she answered Tracy's question. "I'm fine. It's Judge Barnes and I believe Julie." Her voice dropped to a shaky whisper. Afraid that speaking the words aloud somehow gave them life, she continued, "They think it was that rape defendant, Brian Nichols. The guy I was talking about this morning." Her voice trailed off. No more words would come. Tracy asked other questions for which she had no answers. Solemnly, she hit the off button on her phone and dropped her chin to her chest.

The same questions that haunted everyone else that morning haunted her as well. The difference in her nightmare, however, was that she and Gayle had ignored an additional warning. She could not stop her mind from repeating the same phrase over and over again, "His friends knew all along! If only we had said something to the Judge. If only we had said something." Losing herself in her own thoughts, she put her hand up against the wall and leaned her forehead on her arm. Fighting a tornado of emotions spinning around in her mind, she said to herself, "I had no idea he would *do* this!" Lisa's mother let out a slow moan of grief, and Cindy remembered that the time would come later for her personal sorrow. At that moment, her charge was to protect two people who were in grave danger if Brian Nichols happened upon them.

Standing on the sidewalk in front of the Government Center, Tracy and Mike stepped onto Pryor Street. Right away, they could feel the sense of urgency rippling through the crowd. As they ran toward the Old Courthouse and through the throngs of people filling the street, a deputy met them on the sidewalk and said, "The shooter is in the parking deck." All three men ran toward the Underground parking deck. Tracy overheard a passerby say that another deputy was shot on the street. When they reached the corner of Pryor Street and Martin Luther King, Jr. Boulevard, Tracy looked to his right and saw an ambulance with a deputy being loaded into the back. He knew that there was nothing he could do to help the injured deputy. He continued running across the street looking for the shooter, unaware that by that time Sergeant Starks was already clearing the third floor of the same parking garage.

Before most other officers arrived on the scene, Starks approached the Pryor Street stairwell door of the Underground parking deck and put his radio earpiece into his ear. He assumed Nichols was in the garage but was uncertain exactly where. He did not want to alert Nichols to his presence by the sounds of radio communications echoing off the walls.

As soon as Starks opened the door to the stairwell, he was surprised to see a woman on the other side. Prepared to meet Nichols at any moment, he instinctively leveled his weapon at her chest. Frightened by her second encounter with an armed man, she threw her hands above her head and said, "He's got two guns, and he went that way." She moved aside to let Starks pass and then hurried away before she unexpectedly happened upon anyone else. Looking in every direction, Starks cautiously entered the parking area. He knew he needed to retrieve his protective vest from the trunk of his vehicle. As he stood next to his car, he continued looking for Nichols. Starks pulled his vest from the trunk of his car and put it on over his uniform. Afterward, he resumed his search throughout the parking deck.

Meanwhile, for Investigator Tracy Baker and the other men running with him toward the parking deck, those adrenaline-filled moments were unlike anything they had ever experienced. Though Cindy had given specifics about Nichols' antics earlier in the week, at that time it was unnecessary for her to give a physical description. As Tracy searched the Underground parking area, he racked his brain for anything she said that might help him identify Nichols. The deputy running alongside Tracy and Mike was the only one with a radio, and as a result, he was the only one with information on Nichols' possible whereabouts. Tracy and Mike stayed on the deputy's heels trying to hear what little information there was coming across his radio. Eventually, they realized Nichols was no longer in the parking deck. What no one knew at the time was that as Sergeant Starks ran into the stairwell entrance, Brian Nichols drove past the garage in a stolen SUV, headed toward Peachtree Street. Within minutes, his crime spree transformed itself from assault and battery to murder and then armed-robbery. The common denominator for all these crimes was his ultimate escape.

Tracy and the others solemnly walked back to the Courthouse. His cell phone rang and it was his wife. "There's breaking news all over the television about a shooting at the Courthouse!" "Yeah. I just finished sweeping the Underground parking garage looking for the shooter." Disgusted and frustrated by the lack of a coordinated search effort, Tracy needed to get off the phone. Before he hung up, his wife asked if he had on his protective vest. He replied that he did not, but he would get it right away. Tracy thought to himself as he hung up the phone, "If this guy is bold enough to shoot a Judge and a Deputy, he wouldn't think twice about killing me."

Back in his office on the seventh floor, Tracy's cell phone rang again and it was Cindy. With his protective vest on, he strapped his department issued side-arm to his waist as he answered. Cindy sounded more focused than before but still upset. She needed him to come to the eighth floor and escort Lisa and her mother to the Atlanta Police Department for questioning. He told her he would be there in a minute.

On the elevator ride down to the ground floor, Tracy could tell the women clearly were afraid, and justifiably so. He assured them that Nichols had fled the area and was not still around the Courthouse. He told the women that another investigator would wait with them while he retrieved a county vehicle to transport them to the Atlanta Police Department headquarters. Moments later, he pulled a black Cutlass with tinted windows to the front of the Old Courthouse and whisked Lisa Robinson and her mother Barbara away.

SHARED SUSPICIONS

Time: 9:45 A.M.
"I learned there were clues all along."

BY this time, we were being told we could not leave our offices or the building. I don't remember who handed down the mandate, but it probably passed through the crowd of people in the office as other information had that morning. Then someone told me that there was more than one victim, and that it was not Judge Goger, but instead Judge Barnes and Julie Brandau. Even though I had taken my suit jacket off earlier, I suddenly felt warm. The air seemed thick, like a hot summer day in South Georgia. The tie around my neck, which up until that point held no significance, suddenly seemed to restrict my breathing. I tugged to loosen it but did not remove it. People around me started getting more and more agitated. The lack of reliable information, along with feeling confined to the offices, with no clue when it would all end, was maddening. Paul Howard wasn't around. The investigators passed through but were too busy to talk. Many of us felt abandoned and anxious. After aimlessly walking the halls, I decided to head back toward my office and find Gayle to tell her the news.

When I saw her standing near the window in her office, the horrified look on her face told me she already knew. Silently, we stood staring at each other, trying through combined will to find any words to speak aloud. She spoke first.

"Who do you think is doing this?"

I shrugged my shoulders and said, "I don't know. Who would want to kill Judge Barnes?" When I heard the news that it was Judge Barnes, I thought it was Brian Nichols, but again I dismissed the thought from my mind. "What if it has something to do with the Ashe case? Even though he didn't personally get death threats, it could still be because of that." Reluctantly, Gayle seemed to consider the possibility. The Ashe case, after all, had received national media coverage, and it was a controversial decision. Gayle turned to her window while I replayed the case in my mind.

Carisa Ashe had originally been my case but because of the unusually large number of expert witnesses, I asked Gayle to join me in the prosecution. Instead of trying the case before a jury, I chose a bench trial before Judge Barnes. It was my hope that he would better understand the expert testimony than would a jury. The Defendant was a young woman charged in the murder of her four-week-old baby. By the time of the killing, she was already a mother to four other young children. My theory for the motive of the killing was that the thought of raising another child was too much for the young, under-educated, unemployed mother to handle. I urged Judge Barnes to see her as the stressed, overwhelmed young mother with limited options that she was, rather than as the well-coached witness who took the stand during trial. I argued forcefully for a guilty verdict on the charge of murder.

For all who knew Judge Barnes, he was a sympathetic jurist, but he still held some antiquated views about women. He often joked with me about how some women judges and lawyers whispered behind his back that he was a chauvinist. Admittedly, he was full of old Southern ways but was not exclusively guided by them. His thought process was a study in contradictions and was as progressive as it was static. As a result, it was inconceivable to him that Carisa Ashe *could* have killed her helpless child. In his world, women did not kill their children despite countless news stories that suggest otherwise. I could tell he struggled with that reality and feared he might not convict her at all. He ultimately found Carisa Ashe guilty. His returning a guilty verdict and the sentence imposed on her stand as evidence of the two worlds in which he lived. After finding her guilty of the lesser charge of manslaughter, he imposed sterilization as her sentence. The sentence was originally my idea, and I had to convince him it was appropriate. My only motivation as the lead prosecutor was that Carisa Ashe not be allowed to kill another child. I knew that if he found her guilty of the lesser offense of manslaughter, she would not serve a long sentence. I also suspected, based upon her life choices to that point, that becoming pregnant again was highly likely, which meant another child could be in danger.

Once word spread of the decision, groups in every corner of the women's rights and pro-life movements blasted him. Judge Barnes held his ground despite being accused of adopting a paternalistic attitude reminiscent of the Jim Crow South and of setting the cause of equal treatment of women back thirty years. On the day of the sentencing, with Gayle out sick, Judge Barnes and I again discussed the decision at length and agreed it was the best alternative available. Shortly after the verdict, District Attorney Paul Howard received death threats denouncing his role in the controversial ruling.

As I watched Gayle stare out of her office window that morning, I wondered what she was thinking. Like Investigator Cindy Williamson, Gayle's part in the unfolding nightmare was more pronounced than I knew. When Gayle turned around, she said, "What if this is because of Nichols?" It was a possibility we had to consider aloud. We stood silently in her office for a moment lost in our own thoughts.

Months after the shootings, I found out that the week of the killings, one of Nichols' friends had come to Gayle and Cindy expressing concern about Nichols. He told them Nichols would attempt to escape from the courtroom. The friend said Nichols wanted him to conceal a credit card in the suit jacket Nichols was to wear to court on Thursday, the day before the shootings. The friend was so concerned about what Nichols would do, he was afraid to come to court at all that week. What Gayle had no way of knowing at the time, was that she and Cindy were not the only ones to be warned of Nichols' plan to escape. During the first trial, Nichols' mother Claritha e-mailed warnings to Fulton County Deputy Jerome Dowdell whom she knew because they attended church together. She told him she believed Nichols would try to grab a deputy's gun and shoot his way out of the courtroom. Deputy Dowdell, instead of passing such crucial information along, chose to visit Nichols' jail cell and convince him to think of his family and those who loved him. The Deputy believed that praying with Nichols was enough to stop him from acting out his intentions.

There is no doubt in my mind Gayle assumed what she knew was insignificant. Particularly since after the shanks were discovered in Nichols' shoes on that Wednesday, the Judge ordered extra security on that Thursday for delivery of the verdict. Instead of telling anyone about the tip, she focused her attention on ensuring a guilty verdict. In retrospect, her decision to stay silent must have felt sinister, almost criminal.

I looked at Gayle, dropped my head, and walked away. I needed to call Suparna and tell her the news. I knew she would take it hard because she worked closely with both Judge Barnes and Julie for two years.

• • •

Time: 9:48 A.M.
"I placed my 3rd call to Suparna."

As soon as she answered the phone, I could tell she was upset. I assumed she knew, but I said it anyway, "It was Judge Barnes and Julie." At that point, we still didn't know they were dead. I feared they were, but I hoped I was wrong.

Suparna said, "Where are you now?"

"I'm still in the office. For some reason they're telling us we can't even leave. It's crazy around here and nobody seems to be in charge. I'll call you back later. Stay by the phone."

I ended that phone call as I had all the others that morning, without even saying good-bye. I was reeling from the non-stop tragic news, which seemed to be coming at me from every direction. There was a sense that one of the only safe and secure areas in the entire Courthouse was our office. People were too nervous to sit still, but too anxious to stand in the same area for long. The numbers of investigators, sheriffs, and police officers seemed to multiply exponentially by the second. It was common to see law enforcement in the office on a daily basis, but the volume and their somber faces that morning made me and everyone else feel matters would get worse before they got better.

FEARS CONFIRMED

Time: 10:05 A.M.
"I realized my family was in danger."

I WANDERED back into the halls and aimlessly moved through the crowds of people clustered in groups talking amongst themselves. I noticed one group of people in particular gathered around Brad Malkin. Malkin, a District Attorney with the White Collar Crime Division, was animatedly telling the story of what he saw occur on Martin Luther King, Jr. Boulevard from his office window. "I heard this rapid fire 'pop' sound. I thought it sounded like a firecracker at first. Then I heard a bunch of brakes screeching and horns blowing. I got up and looked out my window and I saw a guy running across the street pointing a gun at random cars trying to get people to stop. I saw him jump in a car and speed away. Then I looked down to the sidewalk beside the building and saw a crowd of deputies around another deputy lying on the ground." Malkin kept talking to the crowd but I turned away. I kept asking myself, who could be doing this? Every time the thought came to mind, my subconscious answered "Brian Nichols."

Leaning against a wall, I saw a police officer I did not

recognize swiftly walking toward me while talking into his shoulder radio. Just before the officer reached me he said, "Black male, approximately six feet two inches tall and 200 pounds." There was no more room for speculation. Brian Nichols had shot my friends in the courtroom above me and apparently shot a deputy on the street below. I assumed the unknown officer was coming to me to get a picture or other specifics about Nichols. I was taken aback when he walked by without saying a word to me. I felt numb and needed to find the only other person I thought would understand exactly how I felt. As soon as I walked in Gayle's office, I knew she knew Nichols was behind it all. Without saying a word, I walked out of her office and across the hall into mine. I needed to call Suparna, but decided to wait until I had more information. Word quickly spread through the office that the shooter and the Defendant from our case were one in the same. I don't recall any particular question or response, but it seemed like people bombarded us with hundreds of questions at the same time.

At some point, Cindy and I wandered into each other's paths in the hallway outside of my office. She was upset and I could tell by looking at her that she had been crying. We shared the painful nod which had become the way of saying hello that morning. As we leaned side by side against the wall, we each were lost in our own thoughts. She broke the silence with, "His friends knew. They knew all along what he was going to do." Before I could process what she said, another attorney motioned for me to come to her office and sit down. Without thinking, I peeled myself from the wall, walked over to her office and sat down in a chair. I don't remember anything she said to me or why she thought I needed to sit down. Thinking back, people probably could see on my face the fear and anxiety I was feeling.

Moments later, I looked up just as District Attorney Paul Howard walked by and into Gayle's office. Everyone knew Gayle and I were trying the Nichols case together, and I assumed that when he left Gayle's office he would come to mine, but he did not. At the time, I was distracted by the unnerving events and ignored the slight. It was time to call Suparna again.

• • •

Time: 10:25 A.M.
"I placed my 4ᵗʰ call to Suparna."

"It must have been Nichols who did the shooting."
"Do they know where he is yet?"
"I don't think so."
With each call, I grew more and more anxious about my family's safety. Suparna tried to reassure me that certainly by that time Nichols was somewhere crossing the state line, and outwardly I agreed.

She said, "He wouldn't remain in the city. He knows everybody is looking for him, and he's long gone by now." She told me later that while we spoke, she found herself periodically checking the front windows for any strange cars or people. In hindsight, what she said to me over the phone and what she did were inconsistent, but nothing about that morning made sense.

"You're probably right about him leaving town. I'll call you back later."

• • •

Just that quickly, Ash was gone again and Suparna was left alone to deal with emotions too difficult for her to come to terms with or comprehend. People were calling her and asking if she was okay. She told them she was, but with each call from Ash, she was forced to repeatedly confront the danger her family faced. She was tired of recounting the facts of the tragedy every few minutes. It was not only horrible that her friends had been shot. but the fact that it occurred in the courtroom was unfathomable.

Suparna flopped down into the office chair and laid her head against the headrest. Closing her eyes, she started replaying different conversations from that week in her mind. She thought about the last time she had seen Judge Barnes and Julie. It had been the day before, and she wondered if she ever would see either of them alive again. Thinking of the Judge and Julie made her think about the re-trial, and the argument she and Ash had that Sunday before the trial started. She thought to herself, "What if Ash had been in the courtroom? What if the pictures we had taken were the first and last of the four of us together?"

As her emotions were poised to betray her, her son came into the room and said, "Mommy can I have some *marm* milk?" Suparna smiled at her precious baby's struggle to speak clearly and welcomed the reprieve from her spinning emotions. She rose from the chair, took his hand, and said, "Sure baby. Mommy will get you some warm milk." When she got up from the chair, she bumped against the desk. The computer screen saver that

had turned dark due to lack of activity suddenly came to life
with a large picture of Judge Barnes sitting on the bench.

• • •

As I was aimlessly wandering the halls of the D.A.'s office,
I happened upon an Investigator with the Sex Crimes Unit
named Calvin Thomas. I recalled overhearing someone mention
that Calvin had been inside the courtroom, and I assumed he
knew how Julie and the Judge were doing. I walked over to him
and asked if they were okay. When he didn't respond, I knew
the answer. I felt like I was stuck in the center of a recurring
nightmare and wished I could wake up. I had the terrifying
feeling that everything around me was spinning out of control
and I was helpless to stop it. Knowing Judge Barnes and Julie
were dead, the picture of what was happening crystallized in
my mind. Brian Nichols was on the run and killing people
associated with his rape trials. He killed the Judge and the Court
Reporter. I knew Gayle and I had to be on his hit list. No sooner
had the thought entered my mind, than I ran into Detective
Wade Yates. A seasoned veteran of the Sex Crimes Unit, Yates
was the lead Detective in the Nichols rape case. He testified in
the first trial and was to be the next and last witness to testify
for the Prosecution that morning. As I walked closer to him, I
realized he was on the phone. I overheard him say, "Go to the
school, pick up the kids, and take them home." At that moment,

the reality of the danger my family faced was palpable. I started to think about how shrewd Nichols was. The questions tumbled through my mind faster than I could process the answers. Did he know my full name and address? Did he know what type of car I drove? Did he know what school my kids went to? Did he know that Suparna was my wife? I felt the need to call her immediately.

• • •

Time: 11:05 A.M.
"I placed my 5th call to Suparna."

When she answered the phone, I blurted out that Judge Barnes and Julie were dead. I felt terrible that I had to be the one to tell her the horrible news. She was silent and I kept talking, afraid that if I didn't tell her everything I knew immediately, she and the kids would be in greater danger.

"It's possible Nichols is still in town and may be looking for me and Gayle. Where are the kids?"

"What makes you think that he would even know or remember your name? They're both home from school today. Why?"

"He had the transcript from the first trial and it has my name on it. I'm concerned he might know where we live. One of his friends sells real estate, and he could have told him. Who knows? I don't think you and the kids should be at the house."

"Well, I still think he's half way to Alabama or Florida by now, but we can go to my parents' house."

"We may need to stay there for a day or two, so pack some things. I'll get there as soon as I can, but I want you guys to get out of the house."

"I can have the Nanny take the kids, and I'll wait here for you."

"Okay, I'll call you when I'm on my way."

After that conversation, I hung up the phone and sat solemnly in the chair in my office staring at the two obligatory office décor pictures of my kids and my wife in her wedding dress. How could anything I had done put them in danger? For the first time that morning, I had the very distinct feeling of regret and wished I had never become involved in the Brian Nichols case. I turned away from the smiling pictures on the bookshelf next to my desk and noticed two EMT workers walking toward my office. I thought their presence strange, but the entire morning had been a series of surreal events. The two men walked into my office and said they needed to examine me. I declined, saying I felt fine, just a little shaken like everyone else. One of the workers asked me to indulge them while they checked my blood pressure anyway. I was shocked when they told me that my reading was 150 over 110, because I knew my resting heart rate to be 110 over 80. I was obviously under a great deal of stress and never realized it. The workers started packing away their equipment and insisting that if I did not leave the building, they would be forced to take me to the hospital. About the same time, Investigator Tracy Baker stopped at my office door and looked at me. Maybe he heard them say I had to leave, or maybe he could tell by looking at me that staying was the last thing I needed to do. Whatever the motivation, he took charge and told the EMT workers he would get me home safely.

I think he told me to wait in my office or maybe to wait by the elevators. I really don't remember. In any event, I eventually made my way to the elevators and pushed the button to summon it to the seventh floor. As I waited for the elevator to arrive, I drifted away from the morning and thought of how relatively uneventful life had been only the day before. When the elevator bell rang and the doors opened, I focused back on the present but stood still instead of getting on. Even though there were a few people on the elevator and there was plenty of room for me, I didn't move. For some reason I could not move. Just before the doors were about to close, I noticed two friends of mine, Tony Volkadov and Matt Buzzelli standing in the back of the elevator. Both men also happened to work in Judge Barnes' courtroom. They seemed to notice me at the same time I noticed them, and I struggled to look either man in the eye. I felt as though I owed them an apology, but I also felt a sense of shared grief. Although they never said it, their silent stares tossed questions at me I was unprepared to answer. The most obvious being, would any of this have happened if Gayle and I had convicted Nichols in the first trial? I will never know the answer to that question. What I do know is that we failed to convict him then, and now, even though I was blameless, I felt guilty. The doors to the elevator closed, and just as quickly, they were gone. The entire unspoken exchange between us happened in seconds but it seemed like minutes. When the next elevator arrived, I got on and met Tracy at the front of the building.

From the moment I got into the back of his car, Tracy was talking to me but I wasn't listening. All I could think about was getting to my wife and children. Maybe he could tell that I tuned him out, but that didn't stop him from making his point. "This guy is clever Ash. Everything he's done was premeditated. He thinks he's smarter than everybody else. It's just not safe. . ." Only half-listening, I leaned my head back against the seat and watched the downtown skyscrapers rip past my window. I knew

Nichols was bright, clever, manipulative and cunning. I knew all of it, but I never saw this coming.

I remembered how he tried to intimidate jurors and witnesses during the trials with an icy cold stare or manipulate them with his deceptively charming personality. I started thinking about all of the antics he pulled during both trials. One day in particular during the second trial came to mind. On that day, Nichols walked with a pronounced odd limp, which had not been present the day before. One of the deputies's noticed that he had on tennis shoes instead of dress shoes, and thought it odd as well. Court recessed for lunch and Nichols walked over to me while I sat at the prosecution table. He commented we were doing a much better job the second time around. Accustomed to being around defendants and criminals from my days as a Public Defender, I was unfazed by his standing so close to me. I pointed to the transcript laying on the table from the first trial and said, "We know what everybody is going to say." He shrugged his shoulders and a deputy escorted him from the courtroom without any further conversation between us. The deputy who witnessed the exchange, thought his talking to me was too bold and out of place for a defendant. Originally, she was assigned to escort him alone back to the courtroom from the holding cell after lunch. When she recalled how he brazenly strolled over to the prosecutor's table and tried to engage me in conversation, she decided escorting him alone was not a good idea and called for assistance.

Then after returning from lunch, he tried to create a mistrial. Due to a miscommunication between deputies, the two deputies escorting Nichols didn't realize that jurors were gathered outside of Judge Barnes' private chamber entrance. With his hands cuffed behind him and feet shackled together, Nichols pushed his way past the deputies and into the courtyard area where jurors from his trial were seated. Pursuant to Georgia law, jurors should never see a defendant handcuffed or shackled at any time during trial. The theory behind the law is that handcuffs and shackles imply guilt, and would impair a juror's ability to impartially listen to the evidence and reach a fair verdict. Nichols was aware of the rule because he heard Judge Barnes instructing his deputies to avoid the jurors when transporting him during both trials. When Nichols relayed his story of the encounter to his lawyer, he only mentioned that one of the jurors had seen him in handcuffs, not that he had deliberately tried to get the juror to see him. The juror Nichols identified clearly had no idea why the Judge was questioning her. Nichols, in his haste, had selected the wrong juror. It was not a white female who saw him that afternoon, but a white male, and his attempt to create a mistrial failed.

Riding along in Tracy's car, I remembered that he walked over to me that afternoon in the courtroom. I could see the transcript laying on the table. My thoughts turned to Julie. Did he kill her because I pointed to the transcript? I started shaking my head, trying to erase the thought from my mind. Tracy interrupted the soliloquy going on in my head with, "Ash! Ash! Are you listening to me? I think you should keep my gun. If this guy shows up on your door step, blast him away!" I responded, "I'm gonna' pass on the gun." Even in the heart of turmoil unlike anything I had ever experienced, I knew having a gun was not the answer. I could think of too many cases I had prosecuted over the years where if people did not have a gun on them, the situation would have turned out differently. Guns make it too easy to kill and allow the heat of passion to take over, instead of a cooler head prevailing. I didn't know what I would do if Nichols came for my family, but I knew that having a gun simply was not the answer.

Tracy pressed the issue. "Are you sure?" Uncertain of why I was so sure, in light of the fact that I didn't have a plan, I still knew I didn't want a gun. "Yeah. But thanks anyway." We rode the rest of the way to my house in silence. When I opened the front door, Suparna was walking down the stairs. The house was quiet except for the low rumble of the television in the family room. She walked over to me and I put my arms around her. I saw the tears in her eyes, but I was too guilt-stricken to console her. I needed to see my kids. I needed for all of us to be together. At least that way I felt I could protect them if necessary. I also could not look into her eyes. She needed me to be strong for both of us, but at that moment, I was afraid. Afraid I might see blame in her eyes, and afraid she would see guilt in mine. I pulled away and said, "We gotta' get out of here."

We eventually made it to my in-laws' home, but I remained on edge. They only lived in the house for a few months out of the year, so there was no cable. As a result, we had to rely on people calling us to give news updates, and each time the phone rang, I grew more and more fretful. I was a ball of nervous energy — pacing around the house, constantly checking the time, talking on the phone and watching the windows for any strange activity. It was only noon, but I felt wired, like I had been awake for days.

PROSECUTION EXHIBITS

PART V

The following are copies of the actual exhibits used during Brian Nichols' first and second rape trials.

E-mail from Lisa Robinson to Claritha Nichols requesting help.

08/11/2004 08:25 AM

To: "Claritha Nichols" <
cc:
Subject: Need your help

Hi Mrs Nichols,

I really need your help and to talk to you. I hate (again) to have this conversation over email but I have to. Things between Brian and I are spiraling out of control. The bottom line is that I told him I wanted time and space apart.....that he is open to date other people and me too.

sit on w/stand

Well, I went out to dinner on Mon night with one of the ministers (Chris) from our church (you probably don't know that Brian stopped going to the church about a month ago)...just a friendly dinner but I knew that I was going to let Brian know specifically about Chris because of the fact that he knows him. Anyway, after dinner, Chris stopped by my house on his way to work and Brian was in my room (I didn't know he was there and there were no lights on) and before Chris and I even made it into the front door good Brian was down the steps. He became physical but luckily Chris didn't respond likewise so it was not as bad as it could've been. Brian was definitely out of control and I was very uncertain as to what he was going to do. I was able to calm him down after awhile and we talked a bit, but his anger took over for about 20 min that night.

Yesterday, Brian was calling to let me know that Sonya was now planning to have an abortion and he hoped that this could be the thing that salvaged our relationship. I told him I really thought things were too far gone, I'm unsure that I have the energy that it will take to climb out of this hole, and right now, I just want some space and peace in my life. I need to take care of ▓▓first this time. He's not handling this very well and has indicated that he would rather not live than to live without me. I had to call 911 last night to submit his car / license tag because he told me he was going to end his life and asked me to take care of Whoadie. Then he hung up and wouldn't answer any calls. I left the house to go look for him but couldn't find him. All I could do was pray. I called several times and kept leaving voicemail and text messages to let him know how much everyone (me, you, God, etc) loves him and to not hurt himself. As you can imagine and are probably feeling right now, this was an extremely nerve-wrecking couple of hours. He finally called me and I convinced him to come to my house. The only way, however, that I could convince him was to indicate that there was a possibility for us to get back together. He would not come otherwise. He really wasn't in good shape emotionally when he came to the house. I can't honestly say that we can get back together right now (might happen in the future but now I'm just tired), but I told him that anyway to get him to come to my house. He said he was at the train station. I want to make sure he is 'ok', gets some help, etc. to deal with this. I didn't know what else to do last night and my number one concern was for his safety. I need your help as to what you think I should do. Is there someone in Baltimore that can help? Should I force him to go into a hospital for evaluation/monitoring? My mom was helping me last night and also left him several messages. She thought it was also important for me to let you know. I'm sorry that it has to be over email. Brian doesn't know that I'm emailing you and I'm just trying to keep everything as stable right now as possible. I think all the stress of Sonya, the baby, our relationship, seeing me with someone else, etc. has taken its toll. He may just need to get away to heal....can I put him on a plane to Africa :-) for a few months? He's obviously strong enough to handle this but he doesn't know / feel it right now.

8 days later she want to frame him?

If you want to talk to me directly, please call me on my cell ▓▓▓▓▓▓

(phone)
(fax)

E-mail response from Claritha Nichols to Lisa Robinson

(phone)
(fax)
"Claritha Nichols" <

"Claritha Nichols"
<
08/11/2004 08:46 AM

To:
cc:
Subject: you got it

Thanks ▓ for letting me know what's happening. Isn't it strange how it is so hard for a man to accept you seeing someone else, yet expect you to understand when he sees someone else. That being said, let's get down to business..Is Brian still in Atlanta or did he go to Baltimore. is he still working. Is he using drugs.

He has a best friend in Balto. Zack ▓ and if you can get a hold of him, he may be able to help greatly. The numbers I have for him are home ▓ office ▓ and pager ▓. Zack knows a bit about the mental health field.

How much of all of this is Drama or do you think Brian is serious. Can Pastor Moore help. I suggested to Brian before that he should talk with Pastor Moore or Pastor Lovelace. I would call on one of them at this time because they know both of you and will not need much time to get to the heart of the problem.

You are right that you have to take care of yourself right now and perhaps all of this is to try to put you on a guilt trip. Don't fall into that trap. Suggest that he get help. You are there to help him receive it and after the help then the two of you can talk about salvaging the relationship, but right now each of you need to heal yourselves. tough love. let me know..you know we love you and I really appreciate what you're trying to do to help him. but now he has a chance to see what infidelity feels like and I think it was a good experience for him. If he wants to come to africa , that's fine, but I think he needs to face his problems now..luv you..keep me posted. I don't have international calling privileges..our land line number is ▓.not sure how you dial from the states.

SEARCH WARRANT

IN THE <u>MAGISTRATE</u> COURT OF <u>FULTON</u> COUNTY
STATE OF GEORGIA

Docket No. 2004mN8-9

TO: ALL PEACE OFFICERS OF THE STATE OF GEORGIA

Affidavit having been made before me by <u>LT. JAMES R. LEE</u>, an officer charged with the duty of enforcing the Criminal Laws, that he has reason to believe that in <u>FULTON</u> County, Georgia on the following described person, premises, or property: (state detailed description of person, property or location)
TWO AUTOMOBILES-
A 1994 GREEN CADILLAC ELDORADO, GEORGIA TAG- 571-GNN, VIN- ▇▇▇▇▇▇, THE VEHICLE IS REGISTERED TO CLARITHA NICHOLS OF ▇▇▇▇▇▇▇ JONESBORO, GA. 30328
A 1991 WHITE, BMW 750 IL, GEORGIA PRESTIGE TAG- VRUN12, VIN- ▇▇▇▇▇▇▇ THE VEHICLE IS REGISTERED TO BRIAN NICHOLS ▇▇▇▇▇▇▇ ATLANTA, GA. 30328

BOTH VEHICLES ARE CURRENTLY UNDER THE CUSTODY AND CONTROL OF THE FULTON COUNTY POLICE DEPARTMENT AT 4701 FULTON INDUSTRIAL BLVD, ATLANTA, GA.

There is now located certain instruments, articles, person(s), or things, namely: (specify evidence, contraband or person(s) to be searched for)
ANY HAND GUN, MACHINE GUN OR PISTOL, ANY AMMUNITION OR PROJECTILE, DUCT TAPE AND/OR PACKAGING FOR DUCT TAPE, ANY CONDOMS AND/OR PACKAGING FOR CONDOMS, CLOTHING TO INCLUDE GREEN SHORTS, BLACK T-SHIRT WITH THE WORD "RANGER" WRITTEN IN YELLOW, WHITE TENNIS SHOES, UNDERWEAR, ANY ITEM WHICH APPEARS TO HAVE A SEMEN, BLOOD STAIN, OR HUMAN TISSUE, ANY WRITTEN DOCUMENTATION REFERENCING THE PLANNING OF THIS ATTACK OR THE NATURE OF THE RELATIONSHIP BETWEEN THE VICTIM AND THE SUSPECT, ANY RECEIPT OR RECEIPTS DOCUMENTING THE PURCHASE OF ANY ITEM WHICH COULD BE ASSOCIATED WITH THIS INCIDENT.

Which is (name the law being violated)
RAPE - O.G.C.A. 16-6-1
AGGRAVATED SODOMY- O.G.C.A. 16-6-2
FALSE IMPRISONMENT- O.G.C.A. 16-5-41
BURGLARY- O.G.C.A. 16-7-1

Based upon the affidavit given under oath or affirmation and all other evidence given to me under oath or affirmation, I am satisfied that there is probable cause to believe that a crime is being committed or has been committed and that the property described above is presently located on the person, premises, or property described above.

You are hereby commanded to enter, search and seize within ten (10) days of this date the person, premises, or property described above. A copy of this warrant is to be left with the person searched, if no person is available, on the premises or vehicle searched, and a written return, including an inventory of any things seized, shall be made before me or a Court of competent jurisdiction without unnecessary delay after the execution of this Search Warrant.

SO ORDERED this 27 day of August , 20 04 , at 9:16 A. M.

Sutonia Moran

JUDGE OF THE Magistrate COURT
Fulton County

2004mN 8-9

The facts tending to establish probable cause that a crime has been, or is being committed and the above described instruments, articles, or things described above are presently located at the above described premises or property are as follows: (state in detail the facts that you believe create probable cause, including statement of ownership, possession, or contraband, or person(s) to be searched for.

ON AUGUST 19, 2004, AT 2020 HOURS FULTON COUNTY POLICE RESPONDED TO A RAPE CALL AT NORTHSIDE HOSPITAL. THE VICTIM, ███████████████, STATED HER EX-BOYFRIEND, BRIAN NICHOLS, BLACK MALE, DOB- 12/10/71, ENTERED HER RESIDENCE ON 08/19/2004 AROUND 5:00 A.M. AND RAPED AND SODOMIZED HER. THE VICTIM'S RESIDENCE IS LOCATED AT███████████████████, ATLANTA, GEORGIA, 30342. THE RESIDENCE IS LOCATED IN THE UNINCORPORATED PORTION OF FULTON COUNTY. THE VICTIM STATED THE SUSPECT, BRIAN NICHOLS, ENTERED HER RESIDENCE ARMED WITH SILVER, SEMIAUTOMATIC HANDGUN, THREATENED HER LIFE, BOUND HER WITH DUCT TAPE, AND TOOK HER FROM THE BEDROOM INTO THE BATHROOM AND PLACED HER IN THE BATHTUB. THE VICTIM STATED THE SUSPECT LEFT THE RESIDENCE AND RETURNED ARMED WITH A MACHINE GUN. THE VICTIM STATED THE SUSPECT BEGAN TALKING ABOUT THEIR RELATIONSHIP. THE VICTIM STATED THE SUSPECT THEN FORCED HER TO COMMIT SODOMY BY FORCING HER TO PERFORM ORAL SEX ON HIM. THE VICTIM STATED THE SUSPECT THEN TOOK HER BACK TO THE BEDROOM WHERE THE SUSPECT RAPED HER BY FORCING THE VICTIM TO HAVE INTERCOURSE AGAINST HER WILL. THE VICTIM STATED THE SUSPECT USED A CONDOM DURING INTERCOURSE AND AFTER THE ASSAULT FORCED HER TO SHOWER TWICE. DURING THIS ASSAULT THE VICTIM STATED THE SUSPECT THREATENED TO KILL THE VICTIM, HER FAMILY, AND HER CURRENT BOYFRIEND IF SHE NOTIFIED THE POLICE. THE VICTIM STATED DURING THE INCIDENT THE SUSPECT DRANK RUM AND SMOKED MARIJUANA. THE VICTIM ADVISED HER HAND WAS CUT DURING THE ASSAULT. THE VICTIM ALSO STATED THE SUSPECT BROUGHT A SOFT SIDED COOLER WITH HIM TO THE INCIDENT LOCATION. THE COOLER CONTAINED SANDWICH MEATS AND ICED TEA IN A HALF GALLON CONTAINER. THE VICTIM ADVISED THE SUSPECT FLED THE INCIDENT LOCATION IN HIS GREEN CADILLAC ELDORADO, GA. TAG- 571-GNN.

DETECTIVE WADE YATES INTERVIEWED THE VICTIM AT NORTHSIDE HOSPITAL AND THE VICTIM GAVE DETECTIVE YATES PERMMISSION TO RETURN TO HER RESIDENCE AND PROCESS THE CRIME SCENE. UPON RETURNING TO THE RESIDENCE DETECTIVE YATES LOCATED A GREEN SOFT SIDE COOLER, A HALF GALLON JUG OF ICED TEA, A CONDOM BOX, A USED CONDOM, A CONDOM WRAPPER, A BOTTLE OF RUM, BLOOD SPOTS IN THE BATHTUB, A PAIR OF SCISSORS WITH BLOOD STAINS ON THE SCISSORS. THE ONLY ROOMS IN THE RESIDENCE WHICH APPEARED IN DISARRAY WAS THE MASTER BEDROOM AND THE BATH WHERE THE ASSAULT OCCURRED. THE CRIME SCENE WAS PROCESSED, PHOTOGRAPHED, AND THE EVIDENCE WAS COLLECTED. DETECTIVE YATES OBTAINED WARRANTS FOR THE ARREST OF BRIAN NICHOLS FOR RAPE, AGGRAVATED SODOMY, FALSE IMPRISONMENT, AND BURGLARY.

FURTHER INVESTIGATION REVEALED BRIAN NICHOLS, THE SUSPECT POSSESSES AND DRIVES TWO VEHICLES. A GREEN 1994 CADILLAC ELDORADO, GA. TAG- 571-GNN, VIN-███████████████, WHICH IS REGISTERED TO CLARITHA NICHOLS OF███████████████JONESBORO, GEORGIA. THE SECOND VEHICLE IS A 1991 WHITE BMW 750 IL, GA. PRESIGE TAG-VRUN12, VIN-███████████████, WHICH IS REGISTERED TO BRIAN NICHOLS AT███████████████, ATLANTA, GEORGIA. INVESTIGATION REVEALED THE GREEN CADILLAC IS THE VEHICLE WHICH THE SUSPECT DROVE WHEN HE LEFT THE INCIDENT LOCATION AFTER THE ASSAULT. IT IS BELIEVED THIS VEHICLE MAY CONTAIN THE AFOREMENTIONED EVIDENCE RELATED TO THE CRIMES OF RAPE, AGGRAVATED SODOMY, FALSE IMPRISONMENT, AND BURGLARY. ON 08/20/2004 THE CADILLAC ELDORADO, GA. TAG 571-GNN, WAS LOCATED AT███████████████PARKED AND UNATTENDED. DUE TO THE EXIGENT CIRCUMSTANCES CREATED BY THE MOBILITY OF THE VEHICLE AND THE BELIEF EVIDENCE OF THE CRIME COULD POTENTIALLY BE DESTROYED, THE VEHICLE WAS IMPOUNDED TO THE MAJOR CASE DIVISION IN ORDER TO BE SECURED UNTIL A SEARCH WARRANT COULD BE OBTAINED.

2004mN8-9

ON 08/21/2004 A SEARCH WARRANT WAS OBTAINED FOR THE RESIDENCE OF BRIAN NICHOLS, ███, ATLANTA, GEORGIA. THE SEARCH WARRANT WAS SERVED AT 1920 HOURS. AMONG THE ITEMS RECOVERED IN THE SEARCH WAS A SOFT SIDE COOLER, A ½ GALLON JUG OF ICED TEA, A BROWN WOODEN RIFLE GUN STOCK, AMMUNITION, AND A RIFLE CASE. BRIAN NICHOLS WAS NOT IN THE RESIDENCE AT THE TIME THE WARRANT WAS EXECUTED.

ON 08/23/2004 AT 1750 HOURS THIS OFFICER RECEIVED INFORMATION THAT BRIAN NICHOLS MAY BE LOCATED AT THE CRUNCH FITNESS CENTER IN BUCKHEAD OFF PIEDMONT ROAD. THIS OFFICER WENT TO THIS LOCATION AND LOCATED THE WHITE 1991 BMW 750IL, GA. PRESTIGE TAG- VRUN12. THE VEHICLE WAS LOCATED ON THE TOP DECK OF THE PARKING LOT. THIS OFFICER SUMMONED THE CITY OF ATLANTA POLICE DEPARTMENT FOR ASSISTANCE AND WHEN BRIAN NICHOLS RETURNED TO HIS VEHICLE, THE BMW 750IL, HE WAS ARRESTED AND TAKEN INTO CUSTODY WITHOUT INCIDENT. THE BMW WAS TAKEN TO FULTON COUNTY MAJOR CASE DIVISION AND SECURED.

THROUGH HIS KNOWLEDGE, TRAINING, AND EXPERIENCE, THIS OFFICER BELIEVES THAT SUFFICIENT PROBABLE CAUSE EXISTS TO SEARCH THE TWO AFOREMENTIONED VEHICLES AND THAT INSIDE THE VEHICLES EVIDENCE OF THE AFOREMENTIONED CRIMES EXISTS OR MAY THEREIN BE CONTAINED. IT IS REQUESTED A SEARCH WARRANT BE ISSUED TO FURTHER THIS CRIMINAL INVESTIGATION.

FULTON COUNTY POLICE DEPARTMENT
SEARCH WARRANT EVIDENCE INVENTORY

INVENTORY OFFICER: LT. J. R. LEE _____
FULTON COUNTY POLICE MAJOR CASE DIVISION
4701 FULTON IND. BLVD. ATLANTA, _____
CASE #_2004-840472
1991 BMW 750IL, GA. TAG-VRUN12, VIN ███████████ _____

DESCRIPTION OF EVIDENCE	LOCATION EVIDENCE FOUND	OFFICER
VOLUNTEER ENTERPRISES COMMANDO MARK III .45 CAL SEMI-AUTO MACHINE GUN SERIAL # 19343, LOADED WITH 31 ROUNDS AMMUNITION	TRUNK	LEE
TAURUS PT-99 AF 9MM SEMI-AUTOMATIC PISTOL SERIAL- TIL08458 WITH SUSPECTED BLOOD STAIN ON PISTOL, LOADED WITH 18 ROUNDS AMMUNITION	TRUNK	LEE
BLACK T-SHIRT WITH "RANGER" WRITTEN IN YELLOW	FLOOR BOARD BACK SEAT PASSENGER SIDE	LEE
PAIR OF GREEN SHORTS	FLOOR BOARD FRONT PASSENGER SIDE	LEE
CASE INVESTIGATOR: W. W. YATES		
COPY OF WARRANT LEFT ON FRONT SEAT OF BWM GA. TAG-VRUN12	THIS WARRANT WAS SERVED ON 08/27/2004 AT 1030 HOURS.	

FULTON COUNTY POLICE DEPARTMENT
SEARCH WARRANT EVIDENCE INVENTORY

INVENTORY OFFICER:_Lt. J. R. Lee_____
FULTON COUNTY POLICE MAJOR CASE DIVISION
1994 CADILLAC ELDORADO, GA. TAG- 571-GNN_   CASE #_2004-840472
VIN-████████████, 4701 FULTON IND. BLVD. ATLANTA

DESCRIPTION OF EVIDENCE	LOCATION EVIDENCE FOUND	OFFICER
AMERICAN EAGLE .45 CAL BOX AMMO	TRUNK	LEE
3 BAGS MARIUANA	TRUNK	LEE
TWO LOOSE KEYS	FRONT CONSOLE BETWEEN FRONT SEATS	LEE
1 PAIR WHITE ADIDAS TENNIS SHOES	BACK FLOOR BOARD PASSENGER SIDE	LEE

CASE INVESTIGATOR:_DET. W. W. YATES_____

COPY LEFT WITH/ON:__FRONT SEAT OF CADILLAC, GA. TAG-571-GNN

THIS SEARCH WARRANT WAS SERVED ON 08/27/2004 AT 1100 HOURS.

AP Image

Deputy Cynthia Hall

The Fulton County Deputy Nichols overpowered to escape custody at the beginning of his killing rampage and crime spree on March 11, 2005.

AP Image

Fulton County Superior Court Judge Rowland Barnes

Judge Barnes was presiding over a civil hearing when Nichols secretly entered the courtroom and executed him.

AP Image

***Former Fulton County Prosecutor Gayle Abramson leaving the
nationwide press conference Ash Joshi refused to attend. Prosecutor
Abramson is escorted by unidentified law enforcement officer.***

AP Image

Commemorative portraits of Sergeant Hoyt Keith Teasley, Rowland W. Barnes and Julie Ann Brandau. The portraits now hang in the halls of the Fulton County Courthouse where all three met an untimely death at the hands of Brian Nichols.

AP Image

David Wilhelm

*United States Immigration and Customs Enforcement
Agent David Wilhelm. Agent Wilhelm was Nichols' fourth
and final shooting victim.*

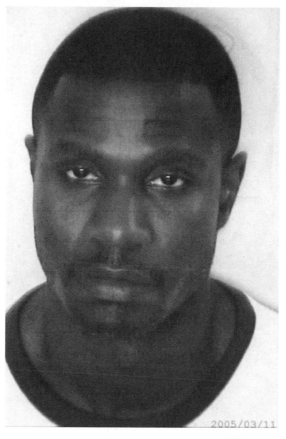

AP Image

Brian Gene Nichols

CITY UNDER SEIGE

PART VI

• • •

Time: 11:31 A.M.

S EVERAL calls, like these below, came into the North Atlanta 911 call center faster than operators could dispatch them to the police.

Dispatcher: "911, What's your emergency?"
"I just saw a black man with a jacket and no shirt walking by Lenox Mall, and I think it's that guy that did the shootings over at the Courthouse."
"Where exactly did you see him, Ma'am?"
"On the side of the mall by Ruby Tuesday's."

Dispatcher: "911, What's your emergency?"
"Yeah. I just saw a black man that looked like that Brian Nichols guy get off MARTA."
"What MARTA location, and was it a train or the bus?"
"It was the train at Lenox Station."
"Thank you for the call sir. Police are on the way to the area."

Dispatcher: "911, What's your emergency?"
"I saw a guy with no shirt on walking by Lenox Mall."
"Ma'am, this line is for emergency calls only. Did the person in the shirt appear injured or in danger or in need of emergency assistance?"
"No, but he looked like the guy all over the television the police are looking for who shot that Judge."
"Where was he when you last saw him?"
"Walking behind the mall near the parking garage."

A Plea to the Public

Time: 4:00 P.M.

BACK on the Courthouse steps, seven hours after Nichols' rampage began, reporters and camera crews from all over the country interviewed bystanders searching for uncovered details of the developing story. They eagerly awaited the start of what would become nationwide scrutiny of the security lapses by the Atlanta Police and Fulton County Sheriff's Departments. News vans with logos identifying various stations with satellite pole feeds extending into the air blanketed the streets and sidewalks around the Courthouse. Several hours had passed since the start of Nichols' crime spree, but the scene around the Courthouse remained frenzied. The police were bothered by their inability to stop Nichols at the Courthouse and were no closer to catching him than they were earlier in the day. Everyone, including law enforcement officials, remained on edge waiting for Nichols to surface or his next crime to be revealed.

Although the Atlanta Police Department spearheaded the search for Brian Nichols, every law enforcement agency in the state was part of the team. In all, some five hundred people were involved spanning from the Georgia Bureau of Investigations, State Highway Patrol, United States Marshall's Service, Federal Bureau of Investigations, Atlanta Police and the Fulton County Sheriff's Departments. Each agency had a representative attend the press conference. Additionally, Georgia Governor Sonny Perdue, representatives from Grady Memorial Hospital, Fulton County District Attorney Paul Howard, and Gayle Abramson also were present. Before the press conference began, Gayle called Ash and told him that Mr. Howard wanted him present in the crowd of officials behind the podium. Ash told her that under no circumstances was he going back to the Courthouse that day, and that he had no plans even to watch it on television. Gayle relented and the two agreed to speak later in the afternoon.

Meanwhile, one of the first people to step before the microphone and vulturous gathering of reporters was Myron Freeman, head of the Fulton County Sheriff's Department. Only on the job for two months, Sheriff Freeman was caught like a deer in headlights by the glaring security lapses on behalf of some of his deputies. Unfortunately, he took over a fractured Sheriff's Department, rife with employee discontent, and a disjointed chain of command. The day's events, which aired the department's dirty laundry for public display, only made matters worse. Additionally, Sheriff Freeman was cut from the mold of a Marine recruit, which was not the type of stilted personality necessary for walking the public tight rope required for such an occasion. Nevertheless, he was the Fulton County Sheriff, and when the people in his department made mistakes, he would have to take the heat for those failings. Before taking any questions, Sheriff Freeman looked at the anxious faces of the crowd of reporters before him. He knew their concerns were the same as every citizen in the city of Atlanta and he shared those concerns. Everyone involved, from Nichols' lawyer Barry Hazen, to law enforcement, was completely blind-sided by Nichols' attack. As Sheriff Freeman prepared to open the press conference, he tried to put what was going on around him in perspective. All of law enforcement must have experienced the same angst in the pit of their stomachs that day as they had four years earlier on September 11th. Until September 11th, no one expected terrorists would fly packed commercial planes into office buildings in New York and Washington, D.C. Similarly, until March 11, 2005, most people thought it inconceivable that a judge could be executed while presiding from his bench in a courtroom. Sadly, the inconceivable on September 11, 2001 and March 11, 2005 had become harsh realities.

Sheriff Freeman began, "We've called this press conference today to ask for the public's help in capturing a fugitive. At approximately 8:45 this morning, Brian Nichols escaped from custody at the Fulton County Courthouse. It is believed that Mr. Nichols then went on a shooting spree inside of the Courthouse. Here is a picture of Mr. Nichols. He was last seen traveling in a green Honda Accord with the license plate number 658 4YN. Under no circumstances should any citizen approach this man. He is considered armed and dangerous." One voice in the crowd of hungry reporters yelled, "Sheriff Freeman! Sheriff Freeman! How did he get out of custody in the first place?" Certainly he expected to receive this question. Nevertheless, he seemed totally unprepared to answer it. Deputy Chief of the Atlanta Police Department Alan Dreher saw Freeman's hesitation and knew the last thing the public needed to see in a time of crisis was its law enforcement leadership unable to react decisively. Dreher stepped forward to the microphone. "The suspect was on his way to the courtroom. It appears that he was — he overwhelmed a deputy sheriff on his way to court, and it appears that he took possession of her handgun. The deputy sheriff was injured as a result of the struggle. The suspect then shot a Judge, and a Court Stenographer, and made good his escape from the courtroom."

A different reporter threw out to the throngs of officials

gathered around the microphone, "Did he kill the deputy and how is he or she doing now?" Another official moved to the front of the crowd, as the others stepped aside to make room for him before the podium. "I'm Dr. Jeffrey Salomone, Head of Trauma Surgery at Grady. A bullet did enter the deputy's skull. She has a small bruise on her brain and some fractures around her face. It appears that after being shot, the deputy perhaps fell to the ground, receiving some of those fractures to her head. She is in critical condition but expected to survive the injuries that she has." In hindsight, the doctor's statements reveal the savage beating Nichols inflicted upon Deputy Hall. Hours later, as the Department Head of Trauma Surgery at the hospital where Hall was being treated answered reporters' questions, he still believed she had been shot in the face. In truth, she had not.

Another reporter asked, "Who's in charge of the investigation and manhunt?"

Deputy Chief Dreher stepped forward in front of the microphone again to speak. "Several law enforcement agencies are committed to finding and capturing this individual. The effort, however, is being coordinated by the Atlanta Police Department. . ."

Al Dixon stood near the rear of the crowd gathered around the podium and reflected upon his last moments in the blood-stained courtroom. He was unable to erase the grisly scene from his mind because he remained in the courtroom until the entire area was sealed and locked. Images of the carnage were seared into his memory, but it still felt as though he were having an out of body experience. He vacillated between grief, the depths of which he had never experienced, and an unwavering determination to gather every shred of evidence necessary to secure a conviction. He found himself picturing how Nichols came through the door, raised the gun, and fired. Until that point in his vision, he could be objective, professional, and even precise in formulating theories to put before a jury. When he envisioned Rowland lifelessly falling to the ground, however, his emotions started to get the better of him.

As the swarm of investigators, police, and sheriffs emptied out of the courtroom, Dixon found himself sitting on the front pew behind the prosecution table. He thought about the last time he saw Rowland alive. Ironically, it had been between the first and second rape trials for Nichols. The two friends talked as they had on hundreds of occasions before. Suddenly, he remembered being in the courtroom during Nichols' first rape trial. He entered the courtroom and waited for the Judge to call a recess in order to discuss another matter with him. Dixon recalled sitting through some of the victim's testimony and tried to remember anything at all about Nichols, but could not. He did recall thinking how Ash and Gayle had their hands full. Trying to convince the jury of an acquaintance rape was difficult, but the victim seemed credible to him. As he refocused on the sea of reporters before him, a cynical chuckle quietly escaped from deep in his throat. The thought that anyone would question whether Nichols was guilty of rape, when killing was obviously so easy for him, was nothing short of absurd. He heard Atlanta Police Deputy Chief Dreher continue to speak to the crowd of reporters.

"At this time Mr. Nichols is not in custody and we still need the public's help in locating him. Thank you to those that have called in with possible sightings. Here is his mug shot again. He was last seen traveling in a green Honda Accord . . ."

The same description of the vehicle Nichols was believed to be traveling in was disseminated to law enforcement agencies around the city and the country. An emergency message displaying the license plate number of the green Honda Accord was posted on Interstate traffic monitor boards across the state like an Amber alert. His mug shot flashed repeatedly throughout the day on television stations across the nation. Dreher continued, "Our officers are out patrolling every square mile of Atlanta and also Fulton County. We have a task force that's working 12-hour shifts looking for this man. He is very dangerous, and still armed."

A reporter for Fox News station asked if there had been a determination of any motive. Paul Howard allowed Gayle, who joined him at the press conference, to field most of the questions about the rape prosecution. He watched her closely and decided that her youth might not have prepared her for the scrutiny her actions would receive later. He moved in front of her to answer the reporter's question about Nichols' motive for the shootings. "I think he probably realized he might be convicted this time. He might not have a chance to walk out. We believe he came here with the intent to make sure that didn't happen." After he finished speaking, Howard moved to the back of the group around the podium. One of his assistant attorneys walked over to him and whispered in his ear. When Howard was certain they were away from the cameras and microphones he told Gayle, "Nichols is still in town. During the press conference, a call came through 911 and they believe it was him. We need to get you somewhere safe for the night."

CALLS UNANSWERED

Time: 4:45 P.M.
"I felt vulnerable and exposed."

SEVERAL of our friends from around the city called Suparna and me on our cell phones while they watched the press conference. They wanted to know if we were watching as well. We repeatedly explained that we were at our in-laws' house, which they used as a vacation home, and as a result, did not have cable. In between answering our continuously ringing cell phones, Suparna and I talked about what we should do next. Friends and family from all over the country called to make sure we were safe. Though I knew Suparna appreciated the concern from family and friends, it was not as helpful for her as it was for me to keep talking about the shootings. My wife is an extremely private person who keeps her emotions to herself, and that afternoon was certainly no exception.

My phone rang again and I guess she could tell by my tone that it was more bad news. Thinking back, I see that she went to great lengths to keep our children from being afraid or having any inkling that something was wrong. I saw her smile at them and then send them out of the room on a scavenger hunt. As soon as they scampered away, she turned to me.

"What is it?"

"Nichols phoned in a death threat during the press conference."

"What did he say?"

I looked away from her because I didn't want to tell her, but knew I had no choice. "He threatened me and Gayle."

"Have they traced the call?" Instantly, her voice was calm but I could tell she was concerned. It was as though I could see the flow chart of questions ticking off in her brain as she tried to anticipate Nichols' next move.

"Debra didn't know that much, but she gave me Paul Howard's Blackberry number and said that I should call him. She thinks that we need security."

"I think we do too. Even though I don't think he knows my parents' names or where they live, he might, and it's getting late. The kids need to eat and there's nothing here for me to cook. I'll order pizza while you call Paul Howard."

I felt her watch me as I walked out of the room to call Mr. Howard. It was like I was in a daze and at any moment I would snap out of it. I just wanted things to go back to normal. I kept thinking to myself, "How could our friends be dead, and my family be in hiding?" None of it made any sense. Pacing back and forth in the kitchen, I placed the first of two calls to my boss' personal Blackberry cell phone. After a few rings, the first call went to voicemail and I left him a message. "Mr. Howard, this is Ash and I'm at my in-laws with my family. Debra called me about the 911 threat, and I think the smart thing to do would be to get someone over here for protection. I'm on my cell, so give me a call as soon as possible."

I went back into the room with Suparna and the kids and tried to think about anything else besides the obvious. Whenever I heard a car door slam in the distance or saw a pair of headlights roll across the room, I would immediately go to the curtains at the front windows. I was afraid for my family's safety, and the reality that I needed to protect them at all costs weighed heavily on me. I thought about where I would tell them to hide and what I would do in case Nichols suddenly appeared.

Almost two hours passed, and Paul Howard had not returned my call. It started to get dark outside. My awareness of my family's vulnerability increased my desire to have armed security at the house. I placed a second call to the personal Blackberry of Paul Howard, but this time I was more forceful than before. "Mr. Howard this is Ash again. This is important. You need to get somebody over here right away. I'm here with my family and we need somebody over here as soon as possible."

When I hung up the phone, I looked at Suparna but before she could look back at me, I turned away. At that moment, the doorbell rang, and my daughter jumped from the floor and rushed toward the door screaming, "Pizza! Pizza!" She reached the door and I yelled, in a tone I had never used with her before, "Get away from the door!" The room fell eerily silent and no one moved. She turned and looked at me with hurt in her eyes and it stabbed my heart. Being my first born, I had spent countless hours staring at those big beautiful brown eyes. I often wondered what was going on in the growing mind behind them, but at that moment, I knew exactly what my daughter was thinking. It made me nauseous to realize that she felt such fear and pain because of anything I had done to her.

I turned to Suparna, who stood as motionless as our son did and said, "We can't stay here tonight. Let's just go to Chattanooga now." We watched them eat in silence and agreed to leave after they finished. Our minivan was parked in the garage with the door down, just in case Nichols knew our vehicles and could identify them. We kept the door closed while we loaded everyone and everything into the van. Suparna and I agreed she should drive and I should sit in the last row of the van. Whether we were being prudent or acting out of paranoia, I can't say. What I do know is that we didn't want to take any chance Nichols might see me on our way out of town. She drove all the way to Chattanooga, while I stayed out of sight.

• • •

Time: 8:05 P.M.

Shaken by the news that Nichols remained in the city and risked being captured to call and threaten her, Gayle welcomed her private security detail. She got into the backseat of an unmarked police car headed for the hotel room she resolved would be her home for the night. Once inside the hotel room, with an armed guard posted at her door, Gayle walked over to the floor to ceiling window and opened the curtain. The sparkling city lights at night were beautiful, but as a prosecutor, she knew of the carnage happening below. Looking out over the city, she wondered about Brian Nichols. Would he be able to escape capture for several years like Eric Rudolph? Rudolph was the man suspected of the bombing in Centennial Park during the 1996 Olympics in Atlanta and the bombing of an abortion clinic in Alabama. He remained on the run for several years before the police were able to catch him. What would she do if the police never found Nichols? Would she spend the rest of her life looking over her shoulder? She felt trapped and alone and thought about the only other person in the world who could understand. She dialed Ash's cell phone and waited with nervous anticipation for him to answer. When he did, he told her he and his family were on the way to Tennessee, and he would call once they settled into a hotel there. Gayle hung up the phone, relieved he was safe and on his way out of town. Alone with her thoughts, she struggled to come to grips with the day's horrific events and wondered if she ever would.

• • •

Time: 12:15 A.M.
"I will never be the same."

After arriving at the hotel in Chattanooga, Suparna and I finally got the children to calm down and drift off to sleep. It was after midnight, and I checked my cell phone one last time and noticed that Paul Howard had not returned either phone call. I tossed the phone on the sofa and thought back to the last time I saw him on his way to Gayle's office. It infuriated me that he thought so little of my family's safety and mine. Even if he assumed someone working at his direction arranged a security detail for us, he could have and should have returned my calls. Refusing to think about it anymore, I closed the door that separated the sitting area of the hotel room from the bedrooms. Suparna looked asleep and I didn't want to disturb her with my last call for the day. I flopped onto the sofa and dialed the number I knew from memory. Uncharacteristically, she answered on the first ring.

"Hey Gayle."

"Hey Ash. Are you guys there yet?"

"Yeah, Suparna and the kids are sleep now."

Lost in our own thoughts, neither of us said anything for several seconds. She spoke first. "If the first jury had convicted him, none of this would have happened!" Her tone surprised me. It was as though she was having a heated debate in her mind, and I came in midway through the exchange.

"I don't know Gayle. Obviously they thought there was reasonable doubt. At least Lyles did."

"Well, I wonder how he feels right about now? I wonder if any of them still have doubt about whether Nichols raped Lisa?"

I understood her anger. Although, because the case was not initially my responsibility, I was able to be slightly more objective. After all, it was the State's duty to prove guilt beyond a reasonable doubt, and obviously we failed. I remembered how I commented to Gayle about Lisa's demeanor during the first trial before I ever joined the prosecution team. I told her that something struck me as odd. I said that if the events she described actually happened, her lack of emotion was unusual, and if I noticed it, certainly the jurors would. I thought about the additional evidence we prepared for the second trial that was never presented during the first. All of the new evidence made the case against Nichols more convincing and would have made a tremendous difference in our favor. Although true, these were not the things my friend needed to hear at that moment. After a conversation filled with long silences, punctuated by brief exchanges, we agreed to talk again in the morning.

I took a long shower and tried to make sense of the day. At 3:00 A.M., drained of every emotion except exhaustion, I lay down. My last thought before I tossed myself to sleep was how drastically life changed for me and everyone around me in less than 24 hours.

UNDER COVER OF DARKNESS

Time: Somewhere between 8:45 P.M. and Midnight

NIGHT started to fall in Atlanta, and Brian Nichols knew that blending in with sports partygoers crowding Buckhead streets after the NCAA Men's Basketball Tournament would be easy enough. They would be less likely to have watched news broadcasts all day and recognize him from his mug shot. Instead, they probably cared more about his pick for the team to win the tournament. Dodging in and out of hotels, restaurants, and public bathrooms helped him allude the stream of patrol cars that steadily whisked past him on the streets near the Lenox Mall. He stole a gray jogging suit and discarded the blue suit jacket and pants he wore during his escape from the Courthouse earlier in the day. Still, he knew his cover as a partygoer would soon fade as the night wore on when the reveling partiers left restaurants empty and retired to their hotel rooms. He needed to get off the streets, but his options were limited. He was certain the homes of his friends would be under police surveillance. Hiding out with any of his "friends" in the drug underworld was not an option either. They definitely would not appreciate the amount of attention his presence could possibly bring. In addition to finding a place to hide, he also needed a car. News reports revealed the police had not discovered the green Honda in the parking garage where he left it and were continuing to search for him in that vehicle. He was several steps ahead of them. Nichols' next moves needed to be swift and shrewd enough to keep it that way. If he stole another car, he would have to keep the victim from alerting the police of his whereabouts. If he had to kill again to further his escape, he would. He resolved to deal with his most pressing issue first. He needed to find a place to hide. He came upon a nearby busy apartment complex and decided it was the perfect spot to look for his next opportunity.

Set back away from the road, the *Summit at Lenox* consists of six large apartment buildings and is deceptively beautiful from the street. Life inside, however, is nothing like the pristine exterior façade would lead you to believe. Often referred to as the "Ghetto of Buckhead," the presence of police cruisers at the complex is a common occurrence. Though it is supposed to be a gated and guarded community, the gates are regularly broken, and the security patrol is scarcely visible.

Around 10 P.M., Iman Adan had just completed her nightly exercise routine in the complex workout facility. Only a few blocks away, she was walking back to her building when she noticed a tall black man in a jogging suit behind her. Initially, his presence did not concern her because there were other people around, walking to and from the buildings. When she reached her building, she entered the security code to release the lock on the door. Before the door could close behind her, Nichols stuck his foot in the door and caught up to her as she got to the stairs. She looked at the attractive man towering over her, then down to the gun in his hand. He said, "I'm Brian Nichols, the one everyone's looking for." Afraid he would take her somewhere else if she revealed that she lived with her boyfriend, she lied when he asked whether she had a roommate. The two walked the three flights of stairs to the apartment she shared with her boyfriend. Iman did her best not to let her fear show. Instead, she tried to figure out an escape, knowing that to try to run away would simply be foolish.

At the door to her apartment, Iman knocked and Shelton Warren checked the peephole. Unclear why his girlfriend was standing at the door with a stranger, he opened the door and she said, "He wants to come in." Shelton looked from his girlfriend's strangely calm eyes to the expressionless eyes of Nichols and then to the gun he had pointed in her side. He moved over pretending he would let them both inside, but instead, pushed his girlfriend inside and Nichols backwards away from the door. When Shelton lunged at Nichols, he lost his balance and fell to the floor. Shelton yelled for Iman to lock the door and simultaneously felt the butt of a handgun collide with his forehead. Nichols pounced on the bleeding man like a wild animal that could smell its opponent's imminent defeat. Shelton's mind swung between two thoughts, "Don't let this guy get in the house," and "God, please don't let him kill me." As Shelton tried to stand, Nichols again struck him in the head, sending blood streaming down his face. Nichols stood over Shelton, angry he thwarted his impromptu plan, but decided not to kill him. The entire attack lasted only a few minutes, and the police arrived shortly afterward but Nichols was gone. Running down Lenox Road, he turned onto the first street he came upon which was Canter Road. Unfortunately for Candee and David Wilhelm whose new home was under construction on Canter Road, Nichols yet again slipped through the grips of law enforcement. It was 10:18 P.M.

Earlier in the evening Candee and David stood in front of their new home and talked about plans for the future. David was a rising star with the Atlanta office of U.S. Immigration and Customs Enforcement. He was promoted to Special Assistant in charge of the Atlanta office, and the couple had recently relocated from Charlotte, North Carolina. While standing outside, they could hear the helicopters overhead and see the large spotlight sweeping across trees and rooftops. Like most others in the city, Nichols being on the loose unnerved Candee. David reassured her of their safety and continued talking about their plans. She listened to him and felt better, because as she often told friends, "living with David was like living with Superman." She left David working on the house and went back to the apartment they were renting in Peachtree City, south of Atlanta. When he did not return home that evening, Candee was not alarmed immediately. Due to the nature of David's job, it was not unusual for him to be out of contact with Candee for short periods of time.

What Candee Wilhelm would later discover is that when Brian Nichols broke into their home, he caught Agent Wilhelm by surprise. When the Agent refused to surrender to Nichols' demands, Nichols summarily killed him.

END OF A LONG DAY

FOR beleaguered D.A. Homicide Unit Chief Al Dixon, it was the end of a tumultuous day. After making an appearance for Paul Howard on the Nancy Grace Show around 9:30 P.M., he talked with crewmembers about the latest in the hunt for Nichols. He wanted desperately to go home. When he got into his car in the parking deck of the CNN Center, he decided to place one last call for the evening to D.A. Ron Boyter.

"Hey Ron, anything new?"

"They found the car."

"The Honda?"

"Yeah."

"Where?"

"In the same parking garage one level below where he took it!" Ron was frustrated with a lax Sheriff's Department that allowed Nichols to escape custody in the first place. Now the Atlanta Police Department wasted ten hours searching for a car that was right under their noses.

"Are you kidding me? So that means we have no idea where this guy is or what he's driving! He could be anywhere by now!"

"Well, reports are still coming in that people have seen him in Buckhead. A couple thinks that Nichols was the man that held a woman at gunpoint and beat up her boyfriend. Although, according to police on the scene, they're having trouble identifying the attacker as Nichols. So you're right. We have no idea where he is. We have local, state and several federal law enforcement agents looking for this guy. . ." Boyter's voice trailed off and his colleague knew exactly what he was thinking. "What if they never find him?"

Dixon said, "I'm going home. Obviously, my phone will be on. There's no telling where he is or what he'll do next. Home's as good a place as any to wait for the phone to ring."

"I'll talk to you in the morning."

Dixon navigated the streets around the CNN building, where the Nancy Grace Show airs, scanning the faces of every person on the sidewalks. He found himself looking for Nichols in every car that passed. He mumbled to himself, "Where are you, and what are you going to do next?" What Dixon did not know, but would later learn, was that around the same time he was leaving downtown, Nichols was calmly driving away from another murder scene. Traveling in a 1994 blue Chevy pick-up truck, with a third gun and the identification badge of a Federal Customs Agent, Nichols was en route to his last stop.

When Dixon finally got home, he could not escape the visions of the lifeless bodies of his friends lying on the floor in the courtroom. That was not how he wanted to remember Rowland and Julie. He struggled to hold on to images of them in life – laughing and joking, both making the people whose lives they touched better. It had been a long eight or nine hours since he was summoned from his home with the call that forever changed his perspective on life. Drained from his emotionally taxing day, he lay down hoping sleep would bring some comfort.

It was not peaceful and did not last long, but sleep eventually came that night.

THE CALLS KEEP COMING

Saturday, March 12, 2005
Time: 10:30 A.M.

THE next day Dixon awakened to sounds from the television in a nearby room. As he lay in bed, he could hear the news reporter talking about the shootings. He tried to block out the reporter's voice and the gruesome images they brought to mind, but he failed. Pulled from his own private hell by his ringing cell phone, he anxiously answered and agreed to the caller's request. Julie Brandau's family wanted to retrieve her belongings from her office at the Courthouse. He told them to meet him there at 11. On the way to the Courthouse, D.A. Boyter called again.

"We've got another body, but we can't tell for sure that it's related to Nichols."

"Where?"

"In Buckhead. A Federal Agent on Canter Road off Lenox. Down the street actually from where the couple said Nichols assaulted them last night,"

"What are the chances that it's not connected?"

"I'd say pretty slim."

"I would too. I'll be there within the hour."

Dixon arrived at the Wilhelm home on Canter Road and police on the scene quickly brought him up to speed on the investigation. Apparently, when carpenters arrived at the Wilhelm residence to resume work that morning, they discovered the deceased body of David Wilhelm on the first floor. He died from a gunshot wound. The Coroner was working to establish the approximate time of death, but it appeared to be somewhere between midnight and about 3:00 A.M. When police officers arrived on the scene, they discovered that his pick up truck, badge, and side arm were missing.

Standing next to a police officer at the Canter Road crime scene, Dixon overheard on the officer's radio that the Gwinnett County Police had Nichols surrounded at an apartment complex. Before Dixon could leave Canter Road headed for the Bridgewater Apartments where Nichols was holed-up, Nichols surrendered. The report over the officer's radio was that he emerged from Ashley Smith's front door waving a white T-shirt. Surveying the number of police officers present, presumably trying to assess his chances of escape, he was immediately taken into custody. As Dixon heard reports of the surrender unfold, he kept thinking Nichols would turn it into a shootout at any moment. Not until he heard that Nichols was handcuffed and in the back seat of a cruiser did Dixon breathe a small sigh of relief.

As the motorcade of cars carrying Nichols and his captors drove through the streets, news helicopters hovered above and roving news reporters scrambled to take the first pictures of the handcuffed man who paralyzed an entire city for 26 hours. Reminiscent of scenes from O.J. Simpson's low speed chase, people, thankful he was in custody, pulled their cars to the side of the road to allow the motorcade to pass. Getting out of their cars, scores of random citizens lined the streets and cheered the police for capturing the state of Georgia's most notorious prison escapee, Brian Nichols. Finally, the 26-hour manhunt was over.

THE RELEASE

Time: 12: 45 P.M.
"I felt relief."

IWOKE up earlier than everyone else did and as soon as I opened my eyes, the fear and dread from the night before returned. I was determined to block out everything going on in Atlanta, and wanted my children to have a good time at the Aquarium in Chattanooga. I can remember them talking excitedly about the fish and plant life. I can't recall, however, whether they were talking to me, and what, if anything, I may have said in response. I do remember walking down a long winding pathway next to an enormous fish tank when my cell phone rang. I recognized an Atlanta area code and moved away from my family, preparing myself to hear more bad news. On the other end of the line, my friend Cathy Lyons, a Sex Crimes Detective, delivered the unexpected news. Nichols surrendered without incident. Like the sound of steam rushing from coffeemakers in Starbucks businesses around the world, the surge of emotions I felt at that moment forced my knees to buckle. To keep from collapsing to the floor, I grabbed onto a nearby handrail. Instantly, I was face-to-face with the gravity of the danger swirling around my family, and its weight nearly delivered a crushing blow to me. I gathered myself and rushed ahead to Suparna to tell her the good news. In the time it took me to walk the 30 steps between us, my phone repeatedly rang with people telling me it was over. When I told her what I knew, I saw relief wash over her tired face.

What I didn't know then but later learned, was that beyond the predictable feelings of relief, my wife bottled up a fury of conflicting emotions. She did say a silent prayer of thanks that we no longer felt like animals in the wild running to save our lives. Her joy, however, was short lived when she thought of the friends she lost and their families. Her grief turned to anger toward everyone who failed to protect them. I appreciate now that the one constant, which held her together during that 26-hour ordeal, was her unwavering determination to protect our children from harm. As I look back, I wish I could have seen her emotional needs, and filled them, but I didn't. Among the other regrets I carry away from this tragedy, my failure to comfort her hurts worst of all. In the final analysis, however, I recognize how fortunate we are to have the chance to move forward as a family. For that gift, I will be grateful forever.

OPEN LETTER TO BRIAN NICHOLS

Dear Mr. Nichols:

Writing this letter to you is one of the most difficult exercises upon which I have engaged. It is, however, an important function as there is much for me to say, and we are likely never to speak in person. Since March 11, 2005, I have had many thoughts about you, ranging from anger and rage, to relief and even happiness. Often this range of emotions occur in a very short period of time, sometimes in the span of a few seconds. Time, though, has a way of tempering extreme emotions, and I suppose that has happened with me. The recurring thought that never escapes me, however, is my absolute inability to understand what you believed your actions would accomplish. Surely, you recognized the folly of the measures undertaken. It is this point I will explore first.

I am a true believer in an accused's right to defend him/herself in a court of law. On that point, I hold no grudges or ill will for the defense you mounted in the first rape trial. In fact, you proved a worthwhile adversary in the courtroom. You handled my cross-examination well, and I have conducted many. You received my questions with little open hostility and responded not to me, but to the jury. You conceded no more than necessary, and did not argue over unnecessary points. In short, you were a very good witness for your cause. While some who read this may be appalled that I do not spew hatred over the fact that your testimony was blatantly untrue, I recognize your testimony to be a by-product of my profession. The court system pits people as adversaries, and when the stakes are great, often one, if not both of the combatants lie to support a position. You are no different. Yes, you lied to the jury, but you felt it was necessary to succeed. This makes you not unique in the context of a trial, but rather common. As a veteran of trial battles, your desperation to win, combined with the stakes of a loss, made your lies almost inevitable.

The second rape trial, however, proved to be a very different matter. Amazing what preparation and knowledge of your defense allowed Ms. Abramson and me to construct. Indeed, I felt the second rape trial was one of the most thorough I ever presented as a prosecutor. We closed off almost all of your arguments from the first trial and presented witnesses who had no bias against you. Your boss from UPS gave irrefutable testimony about the shocking lie you told him about the death of your mother and grandmother, even as he admitted your best qualities as an employee. Your Pastor, a man who professed his love to you, testified that Lisa had moved beyond you, a fact you would not accept. Phone records clearly established that you were not with Lisa at the times to which you testified in the first trial. DNA evidence confirmed that it was blood on the scissors you used to cut Lisa's hands free. It was an excellent case against you in the second trial, and to your credit, you recognized as much and admitted it to me two days before you removed any doubt of your guilt.

This brings us to the pink elephant in the room – your murderous rampage. I understand the desire of a criminal defendant facing almost certain conviction, and any useful years incarcerated, to attempt to escape. Over the years in my career as an attorney, many people have told me they would rather flee than face extended imprisonment. Whether some or any of those people would actually follow through with their stated intention is another story, but at the very least, the thought crosses peoples' minds. It is only natural that the thought crossed your mind; that is not the baffling part. Here is what I don't understand. You had a chance, a great chance, to leave before anyone even knew you were gone. Arguably, you could have been many minutes or even hours ahead of authorities, thereby greatly increasing your odds of extended freedom. As it turns out, however, that was not your goal. You had a chance, and you threw it away to commit senseless and suicidal acts of violence. One thing I know from being your adversary is that you are not stupid. You had to have calculated that the time it took to kill Judge Barnes and Julie Brandau would negatively affect your chances of an undetected escape.

Yet, you did it anyway. Which can lead to only one conclusion — you have an evil heart. You are not selfish, per se, because the selfish act was to escape. Rather, you were intent on causing pain and suffering. Given the opportunity, you would have caused the same pain in my family as you did to those who loved your deceased victims, and here maybe is where I become predictable. I'm unsure of words strong enough to describe my disgust for what you did to my friends, my family and to me. I have imagined tortuous ways of punishing you, envisioning the look of excruciating pain I hoped would cover your face. I've chided myself for having such evil thoughts because I'm not like you. Unlike you, I have the capacity to care for another human being and would never intentionally harm anyone. Unlike you, I have a conscience that guides my actions. Unlike you, I respect our system of justice and the laws that govern our society. Make no mistake, even though my hatred for you is not on constant display, it remains intact. In the end, however, it won't be my hatred for you that will determine your fate, but rather an unbiased group of people representing a system you tried to destroy.

THE AFTERMATH

PART VII

CHARTING A NEW COURSE

June 2005
"I knew it was time to move on."

IWENT back to work on the Monday following the shootings. In hindsight, that was probably too soon. I should have taken some time off, but I couldn't think of what I would have done if I had. I didn't necd more time alone to think through the day's events. That wasn't something that was particularly helpful for me. Instead, I talked about the shootings and faced my responsibility for the part I played. Over the next several months, I tried to tell myself that my work as a prosecutor remained important, but now I knew there were limits to its significance. Prior to March 11th, I never considered that my work could place me or my family in danger. After the shootings, that reality wasn't something I could conveniently ignore or dismiss any longer. After talking it over with Suparna, I decided to leave the D.A.'s office and become a Criminal Defense lawyer. I reconciled the change by telling myself that convincing my client's to accept responsibility for their actions was merely a different side of the same coin from my role as a Prosecutor. Word traveled through Courthouse circles that I was leaving, and it seemed that everyday somebody wished me good luck. As my time in the D.A.'s office came to an end, I had a conversation with one Deputy in particular that reinforced it was indeed time for me to leave.

"Hey Deputy. What's up?"

"Still dealing with all of the fallout from the shootings. It seems like everybody is finger pointing. But what are you gonna' do? I hear you're leaving the D.A.'s office. When's your last day?"

"Thursday." I was aware of what he was talking about because there were at least two separate investigations going on. One being conducted by the Sheriff's Department and the other by a team put together by judges in the Courthouse who wanted answers. It was definitely still tense with various agencies trying to deflect attention from their own failures.

He said, "I guess you need a change of pace?"

I thought about the obvious answer to his question, and wondered whether he could tell what I was thinking. Working in the Public Defender's and Prosecutor's offices for several years, I had come to know most of the deputies who worked in the Fulton County Sheriff's Department. At some point or another, we had crossed each other's paths, and with most, if not all of them, I had a casual yet professional relationship. I knew some of them worked harder than others, but I never got the sense that any of them were down-right incompetent. As I stood there talking to the Deputy, I could not help but think whether there was anything different he could have done that morning to stop Nichols. I also wondered whether he thought the same thing about me.

"Yeah. I tell you the more time that passes and the more stuff I find out, the more disgusted I get. It's just best if I call it a career and move on to something else."

For several months following the shootings, there were news reports in the paper and on television about the shootings and all of the mishaps that happened behind the scenes. There were deputies who said that they were watching the surveillance screens in the control room. In fact, they were off getting breakfast sandwiches. There were deputies who clocked in as present in the building, but were actually working extra paid detail at the Georgia Dome for the NCAA Men's Basketball Tournament. Then there was the deputy who said he passed by Nichols after the shootings, which would have been bad enough, but who really walked by Nichols after he had brutally beaten Deputy Hall, but before he ever got to Judge Barnes' chambers. Since the shootings, county officials spent millions of dollars for additional security measures. I questioned whether the motivation for doing so was to strengthen security or to improve their public image.

Thinking about how county officials handled the backlash turned my thoughts to Paul Howard. Even though I may have disagreed with the way he ran the District Attorney's office, I respected him. Anyone who has worked for him can attest to his micro-management of every single issue in the department. It was the subject of more than one conversation around the lunch table. Still, I respected him as my boss and as a skilled lawyer. He also respected my talents as an effective trial lawyer. When a high-ranking City of Atlanta official was charged with soliciting sex from a 15-year-old boy at the Greyhound bus station, Mr. Howard entrusted me with the prosecution. I talked with him about my ideas for the closing argument. He had a different approach than I, and frankly, I liked his idea better. I can still see him standing in my office weaving the theories of the fundamental equality of all men with the right to receive justice, even if you couldn't afford it. The argument was powerful, particularly since the young boy who was the object of the Official's desires was significantly less than financially secure. I used the argument in my closing and the jury returned a guilty verdict. Regardless of any of those realities, for him to ignore my plea for help and not return my calls that tragic night was just plain wrong. An even greater insult, however, was for him to have the audacity the following Monday morning to say to me, "Let's keep it all in the family. There's no need to discuss particulars in the media." It was just too much for me to tolerate. Did he really think those patronizing statements of a false solidarity would be enough to keep me from telling the truth to anyone who would listen? It was absurd. I knew his private security detail ensured his safety that evening. It wasn't his family whose lives were in danger that night. He wasn't the one who was lying down in the backseat of his family's minivan while his wife drove the family out of town. No. It was me. I was actually afraid that if we accidentally drove by Nichols, he would shoot, and possibly injure or kill any of the three people I loved most in this world. That was my burden, not Mr. Howard's. It was my family, and the lies surrounding that day's events continue to infuriate me.

The look on the Deputy's face led me to believe that I had missed a portion of our conversation while lost in my own thoughts. He seemed to dismiss my misplaced silence and asked, "Did something else come to light I haven't heard about?"

"Well, I don't know what all you know, but when I talk to people and hear about the e-mails and lost reports, I just shake my head. It didn't have to happen. Nobody had to die."

For a split second, I thought I saw the expression on his face change. Was it guilt? Was he one of the ones who knew of Nichols' plan but failed to say anything? Regardless, he probably replays that morning over in his mind a thousand times a day. Irrationally wondering if he could have done anything differently to prevent it, but logically knowing the only person who should bear that responsibility is Brian Nichols.

The Deputy continued, "I was talking to Deputy Jenkins the other day after roll call, and he told me about the day he found the shanks on Nichols. He said that when he told Nichols he was going to search him, the guy didn't even flinch. Nichols had to know that Jenkins would find the shanks in his shoes and that he would get in trouble, but that didn't scare him at all. Jenkins said Nichols just apologized for having them, and remarked that he didn't mean any harm. Nichols even said the shanks were in his shoes for some type of medical problem he was having with his foot. Incredible!"

"I'm not surprised. I'm not surprised."

Regrettably, nothing I learned about Brian Nichols after the shootings, surprised me anymore. As I walked away from the Deputy and into a nearby courtroom, I took my seat at the Prosecutor's table waiting for the judge to take the bench. I flashed back to the day the deputies found the shanks in Nichols' shoes, and him walking over to me in the courtroom. What I didn't learn until later was that one of the deputies thought his coming over to me was too bold. Because of her suspicions, she requested a male Detention Officer search Nichols and that Detention Officer discovered the shanks in his shoes. The Deputy and the Detention Officer who found them, filled out a detailed report of the discovery and passed copies along to everyone in their chain of command. They even made sure the actual shanks and a copy of the report went to guards at the jail housing Nichols. To know all of that happened two days before the shootings, and he was still able to break free was frustrating. Why didn't the guards at the jail search his cell? Why didn't they put him in a different color jumpsuit, as required by department policy, which would have alerted everyone that he was a high-risk inmate? Who assigned Deputy Hall to escort him alone? These are just some of the questions with no logical answers.

Later that same evening, unaware of the shank discovery, Nichols' lawyer Barry Hazen, Judge Barnes, and I were sitting in Judge Barnes' kitchen eating cake. It was such a typical scene for Judge Barnes. His friends and colleagues gathered around food, all the while enjoying each other's company. He found any excuse to throw a party, and that day it was the retirement of another judge's court reporter. At some point in her career, she worked with Judge Barnes, and he took it upon himself to give her a going-away party. The three of us were sitting at the table talking about events in the news and I brought up the shootings of Judge Lefkow's family in Chicago. It was in the news because the public learned the shootings were connected to a case over which Judge Lefkow had presided. I wondered if Judge Barnes worried about his safety in light of what happened to that Judge's family. I asked him and in his trademark cavalier style, he shrugged his shoulders and said, *"You just can't worry about that kind of thing. It's just not something I spend my time thinking about."* Sadly, it was his general belief in the goodness of man which left him vulnerable to the likes of Brian Nichols. If only he had opted for a smaller courtroom and moved to the New Courthouse, Nichols would have had fewer opportunities to escape.

In hindsight, two things about that conversation with Judge Barnes strike me as ironic. First, around the time we were having the conversation, deputies were searching Nichols and would soon discover the shanks. Such a discovery should have triggered a domino effect of increased security measures by the Sheriff's employees which, at minimum, would have made it more difficult for Nichols to escape. Instead, crucial links in the chain of communication faltered, resulting in disastrous consequences. Secondly, the retiring Court Reporter we were honoring with cake worked in the courtroom attached to the holding cell from which Nichols escaped. If she had not retired the Wednesday before the shootings, she would have been in the courtroom Nichols first walked through after leaving the holding cell area. Sergeant John Starks, also assigned to that same courtroom, would have been with her. Perhaps, if they had been in the courtroom, they too would have fallen victim to Nichols' rampage, or maybe they would have been able to stop him. We'll obviously never know, but I can't help but wonder.

Then there was the meeting in Judge Barnes' chambers the morning after the deputies discovered the shanks. Judge Barnes summoned Barry, Gayle, Cindy, and me for a closed-door session. He told us about the shanks and said he would request additional security for the reading of the verdict. At the time, having additional security was protocol for defendants who might react violently to a guilty conviction. Having worked around so many criminals throughout my entire career, neither the meeting nor the need for additional security concerned me. Looking back on that meeting, I wonder what Gayle, Barry, and Cindy were thinking when they heard about the shanks. None of them disclosed that Nichols wanted his friend to conceal a credit card in a suit he was to wear to court. Perhaps if they had, Judge Barnes would have considered Nichols more of a threat. We did talk that morning about whether we thought he was dangerous. I assumed we each were drawing upon our experiences with Nichols over the last several weeks. Nothing I knew at that point led me to believe that he was any more, or less dangerous than most of the criminals I came in contact with daily. Maybe if I had known about the e-mail from his mother, or his wanting the credit card, I would have felt differently. I cannot imagine why neither Gayle nor Cindy mentioned what they knew. I understand how Barry must have struggled with that information, since he was Nichols' lawyer. Bound by the attorney-client privilege to protect Nichols' confidences, Barry had considerations different from Gayle and Cindy. Still, that duty would not extend to criminal acts. Questions about the failures and lapses that fateful morning are never-ending. On some level, the answers don't matter anymore. People died, others of us were traumatized by it all, and no answers can change those realities.

When I heard the bailiff give the universal signal for a judge entering a courtroom, I forced images of Judge Barnes from my mind and re-focused on my task at hand.

An Unlikely Angel?

October 2005
"I couldn't believe the things she said."

S UPARNA thinks I suffer from insomnia. I don't know, maybe I do, but whatever the case, nightly runs to *Borders* have become a regular occurrence for me since the shootings. Several months after the shootings, the mood struck me and I wandered into the store not far from our home. With no particular interest or destination, I walked up and down the aisles trying to burn some energy, glancing at various titles along the way. I passed by one display and the picture on the cover stopped me dead in my tracks. It was a book cover with Ashley Smith sitting in a chair looking homegrown and innocent. Instantly, my entire purpose in the store that evening changed.

Ashley Smith was the woman portrayed as Brian Nichols' final hostage. Allegedly strangers when their encounter began, she claims that she convinced Nichols to surrender. From the moment I heard her incredible tale, it didn't ring true to me. As a prosecutor, gut instincts guide the way I hear people's accounts of events. I am trained to look for inconsistencies in those accounts and determine their significance. For my purposes,

Ashley Smith's story was stock full of facts that at a minimum were untrue, and at worst made her an accomplice after the fact in Nichols' crime spree. My suspicions were further heightened when I talked with several of my friends in law enforcement who were working on the case and learned they had similar concerns. As time moved on, questions about her truthfulness turned into utter disbelief, and Ashley's far-fetched story turned into a book. By then, however, Governor Sonny Perdue, along with the national media had joined the ticker-tape parade in her honor. None of the people who talked to me questioned the reliability of her story in public for fear of backlash by their superiors, but they all wanted it off the front pages of newspapers as quickly as possible.

I took the book down from the shelf and flipped through the first couple of pages. Page after page I found myself struck by statements that appeared to be in capital letters with bold type, though they weren't printed that way. One line in particular leapt from the page and I kept reading it over and over. She says that after he grabbed her by the arm, and forced her into her apartment, all the while waving a gun in her face, he asked her, "Why'd you scream?" According to Ashley Smith, that was the *first* question Brian Nichols posed after allegedly taking her hostage. She says, he asked the question not once, but twice. Her account in the book says she replied, "What? Why did I scream? I . . . I don't know you. It's two in the morning. You have a gun pointed at me. I'm scared!"

Smith's account of that initial exchange between the two of them is not the sort of exchange one would expect between random strangers. Especially, after one has forced his way into the other's home at gunpoint. It is the kind of incredulous question, however, you ask an acquaintance who unexpectedly screams when they see you. The only logical reason Brian Nichols would ask that question was because *he* was shocked that Ashley Smith *would* scream.

By the time her book hit stores, I knew Brian Nichols had confided in a friend that he knew Ashley Smith before that night. As I leaned against the bookshelf, I thought about Nichols and what else he told the same friend. It wasn't just that he knew her, but they also had sex during the night and did drugs together. Yet, she was holding up her story as proof of a religious breakthrough and denying any facts that didn't help her spin. It was only after her book deal that she even admitted she had drugs in her apartment and gave them to him. The truth, however, wasn't something many people involved in this sad story wanted to hear.

Even though it was late, there were other people perusing the aisles, and every so often I would look up and find somebody staring at me. In retrospect, it was probably because I was talking to the book in my hand as if it could talk back. I flipped through another couple of pages and got to the part in her story where she describes with meticulous detail laying out the drugs she gave Nichols that night. I remembered her saying in an interview that her stash of meth was left over from the day before and how getting high on meth gave her the energy boost she needed to move by herself. I kept thinking, "What drug addict *saves* some for the next day?" In all my years of prosecuting and defending drug addicts and drug dealers, I never heard of one *saving* any portion of a hit. When I first heard her admit to being addicted to drugs as recently as the day before Nichols appeared on her doorstep and then deny using them that night with Nichols, I thought her claims were preposterous. Then I thought of what Nichols told his friend about doing the drugs with her that night. He said, "When have you ever known a crack head to sit there and let you get high off their supply?" What his friend claimed Nichols said was certainly more consistent with my experience than her contrived version of events.

I kept reading and saw the passage about her needing a credit card from her purse where she writes, " 'Hey,' I called out to him.

He was still in the bedroom. 'I need my pocketbook.' 'It's in the living room,' he said.'" I shook my head in complete disbelief of the account. How in the world could she expect anybody to believe that a total stranger, who at two o'clock in the morning forced his way into her apartment at gunpoint, would calmly sit in her bedroom while she laid out drugs for him. She meanwhile, casually walked between her bathroom and living room to get her pocketbook, and never once considered grabbing the three guns he supposedly left alone in the bathroom with her or bolting out of the apartment. I remembered watching her interview with a CNN reporter who interviewed several people affected by the shootings. During her piece, the reporter walked Smith through the apartment where she was living at the time. The first point that came to mind as I read her account in the book was how far apart the bathroom and living room were from each other. She easily could have walked out of the front door as he sat on her bed in the back of the apartment.

What should be obvious to any thinking individual is the comfort level he had with her, as evidenced by the fact that he did not find it necessary to stay in the same room with her at all times. While skillfully setting up the drugs and walking from room to room, she makes no mention of thoughts of escape from her alleged captor, nor any mention that he was concerned she might try to flee. Instead, she says her focus was on, ". . . getting the drugs laid out for him so he could make a choice."

What I found even more unbelievable, however, was that she expected people to believe that a quadruple murder suspect, on the run for his life, would develop such a close trusting bond with a complete stranger in under two hours. According to her version of the events, he accosts her, tapes her hands and feet together, takes a shower, and she gives him drugs, all by 3:00 or 3:30 in the morning. I kept saying, "These are lies. Just lies!"

I flipped through another few pages and saw the part where she talks about discovering David Wilhelm's death and about the blue truck Nichols parked outside of her doorstep. She talked earlier in the book about seeing the truck when she first went outside to go to the store, and then noticing it had moved closer to her parking spot when she returned home. She says when she returned to the parking lot outside her apartment, she noticed someone was sitting in the truck and became alarmed. She allegedly started to sweat and thought about going to her mother's house nearby but decided against it. Her sixth sense told her something was wrong while she sat in her car shaking, thinking of what to do next. According to her accounts, her stepfather had called her twice earlier in the evening specifically to warn her about Brian Nichols. Even in light of those warnings, and her sixth sense alerting her to possible danger, she wanted people to believe that she got out of the car anyway!

Even more unbelievable are her actions after she learns the truck belongs to a murdered Federal Agent. By her own admission, she leads the murderer on an early morning journey to stash the truck so police would not find it outside her apartment door. Interestingly enough, before they leave she has the calm presence of mind and vain desire to change her clothes, grab a hair band to pull her hair from her face, and ask him if she can take her cell phone. After they returned from their early morning task of hiding Agent Wilhelm's truck, she made pancakes and eggs for the two of them. She served juice, brought him his plate, and then casually sat down to breakfast with a quadruple murderer. After reading her account of her time with Nichols, I came away feeling like the two were winding down an evening of simply enjoying each other's company and topping it off with breakfast. Yet, she wanted reasonably objective people to believe she was held against her will.

Under Georgia law, a person can be charged with a crime if they meet the statutory requirements of aiding or abetting another in the commission of that crime. I do not argue that she should be charged with David Wilhelm's murder, but there is no doubt she helped Nichols conceal the evidence of that murder by helping him hide the truck. That culpability, however, is not what resonates most with her about her time with Brian Nichols. She does not even describe being preoccupied with escaping from her alleged captor. What hostage, truly afraid for her life, is not constantly looking for any opportunity to escape? Instead, she talks with pride about him referring to her as a "ride or die chick," a reference to a rap song that she told him earlier in the morning was one of her favorites. She proudly describes how he trusts her — after she waited for him to stash Agent Wilhelm's truck, get into her car, and drive him back to her apartment.

The fact that the police could find no obvious connection between the two of them only serves to support the reason he went to her home in the first place. Twice that night, he tried and failed to find shelter in the homes of random strangers. He could not go to his home, Lisa's home, friends' homes or his parents'. All certainly were under police surveillance. There was no place else for him to go. He had to get off the streets before someone recognized him. What better place for him to hide than the least likely place the police would be looking for him? Conspiracy theorist offer several possible scenarios as evidence that Nichols knew Ashley Smith before he suddenly appeared at her apartment that night. Some say the two knew each other from being in a drug rehabilitation facility together. Others posit that the two knew each other from a drug house both used to frequent in Augusta. What I suspect, however, is that a major drug dealer in Atlanta, who uses smaller dealers throughout the state to distribute drugs on his behalf, is the connection between the two. I believe that there were two disciples of that drug lord who kept each other's company. One of those disciples was Brian Nichols and the other was the boyfriend of Ashley Smith. Nevertheless, the fact remains that after going to Ashley Smith's home, Brian Nichols chose to stop killing. For that accomplishment, she does deserve praise, but to overlook the blatantly false and contrived account she offers of those early morning hours is disrespectful to others whose lapses were laid before the world to be judged.

Disgusted, I tossed her book back on the display and walked out of the store. I know that eventually Ashley Smith's account will have to withstand closer scrutiny, and the jury of public opinion will have to decide whether she is to be believed. I have no questions about where I stand on the issue.

OFF THE RECORD

"I just have to get this off my chest."

IN the week following the shootings, my wife and I attended three separate memorial services for Rowland K. Barnes, Julie Ann Brandau, and Hoyt Keith Teasley. Each one distinctively different from the others because of the individual whose life was honored, yet they were similarly connected because of the manner in which they died. The seating was divided at each service between public mourners and the victim's families and close friends. At each service, Suparna and I sat in the private section, and during the service for Judge Barnes, the brave front I had painted for the world to see shattered completely. I don't recall at what point in the program it started to happen, but one thought kept circling around in my mind. "If I had convicted this guy, Rowland Barnes would still be alive." The words swirled around in my mind, while growing louder and louder, until finally, I snapped. When I did, tears rushed from deep within my soul. Until that time, I had not cried. On some level, crying didn't seem like an option when so many people around me were in pain. I felt like I had to stay strong and in control for others who might need my help. On another level, and more poignantly, crying out of grief happens only upon moments of reflection. Until then I had not reflected upon the entire situation. Sitting at the memorial service for Judge Barnes, I reflected on the magnitude of the loss his death caused and my role in it. I felt like I was to blame and the image of Brian Nichols pointing the gun at him dominated every conscious thought. I was inconsolable, and only fleeting rational thoughts of exactly who is to blame for this tragedy were of any consolation.

Like so many others, I struggled to understand how one person could inflict so much harm in such a relatively short period of time and show absolutely no remorse for the pain he left behind. The difference between me and many others who ponder the events of March 11th, however, is that my questions start with "how," instead of "why." Simply put, I answered the "why" questions in my mind early on. In my opinion, Brian Nichols is a classic psychopath and nothing I have learned about him to date has forced me to revisit my conclusion.

I was raised in a home with a family that spent a fair amount of time talking with each other about various issues. As it turned out, one of the more interesting topics of conversations was my mother's work as a psychiatrist treating a variety of mental illnesses. To those who say that my childhood memories do not qualify me as an authority in the field of mental health, I willingly concede the point. I do not believe that my years spent at my mother's knee rival the knowledge of trained professionals in the mental health field. Nonetheless, I do believe that it made a significant difference in my ability to understand mental illnesses in ways most people do not. I was fortunate to be exposed to diagnoses and treatment options within the mental health field in a manner most people never encounter outside of an educational setting. I liken my experience to that of my children. Having two lawyers as parents, and discussing legal issues in their presence, will afford them a level of understanding of the law beyond television's *Law & Order*. Notwithstanding that reality, I would not expect either of them to be able to practice law without formal training.

Ironically, or perhaps prophetically, I graduated from law school and chose a field that offered a human laboratory rife with opportunities to observe, analyze, and hypothesize about the connections between criminal behavior and mental illness. Over the course of my career, first as a Public Defender, then Prosecutor, and now Criminal Defense attorney, I have encountered first hand many of the diagnoses my mother and I discussed over the years. With that history and knowledge, I view Brian Nichols through a prism different than most. I do not see his actions during either trial, or on that fateful morning, as the actions of a "mad man." To the contrary, I see Brian Nichols' actions as that of a psychopath. He selfishly set out to satisfy his own needs and desires without any regard to the pain his actions certainly would cause others.

According to Dr. Robert D. Hare, renowned expert on psychopaths and author of *"Without Conscience: The Disturbing World of the Psychopaths Among Us,"* psychopaths have a grossly inflated view of their self-worth and importance. They see themselves as superior beings who are justified in living according to their own rules. Their astounding egocentricity often emerges in dramatic fashion in the courtroom. Webster's New World Dictionary defines egocentric as viewing everything in relation to oneself. For example, it is not unusual for psychopaths to criticize or fire their lawyers and take over their own defense. This sense of entitlement is one of the hallmark indicators of psychopaths, and Brian Nichols is no different.

During both his first and second trials for Rape, Aggravated Sodomy, False Imprisonment, and Burglary, Brian Nichols never carried himself with the air of a criminal defendant. Usually, people who find themselves thrown into the clutches of the criminal justice system discover a certain level of humility. I have found this to be true even if the individual is innocent, and especially if they are guilty. Such was not the case for Brian Nichols. From the moment he stepped foot into the courtroom, he displayed a perpetual smug grin that bordered on arrogance. For most criminal defendants, especially those charged with rape, that is a dangerous emotion to display. This was particularly true for him, given the gruesome details his rape victim testified about during both trials. Without regard to that fact, he behaved as though he were co-counsel for the defense team, rather than the perpetrator on trial charged with a crime. He actively participated in jury selection, instructing his lawyer on who to eliminate from the jury pool and why. He took copious notes when witnesses testified and routinely, throughout both trials, would get up from his seat at the defense table and hand a note to his lawyer standing at the podium. It is one thing for criminal defendants to show an interest in the process that will determine their fate. However, it is another matter entirely for them to believe they can out wit the prosecution, deputies, the judge, and jury. Brian Nichols fell into the latter category and will no doubt derive a degree of pleasure in learning that I noticed his antics and was powerless to stop him.

As I look back on the robbery and assaults Nichols committed immediately following the shootings at the Courthouse, I find it stunning. Within approximately a five-mile radius and a 15-minute time span, he methodically assaulted and robbed five different people at gunpoint. The single element present in each one of those victims' accounts is his chillingly cold demeanor. Unaffected by the stress of fleeing from police or the terror he inflicted upon his victims, he was fearless and determined to have his way.

According to Dr. Hare, for most of us, fear and apprehension are associated with a variety of unpleasant bodily sensations such as sweaty hands, a "pounding" heart, and "butterflies" in the stomach. We often describe fear in terms of bodily sensations because we feel them when placed in anxiety-filled or scary situations. Dr. Hare describes how fear, like most other emotions in the world of psychopaths, is incomplete, shallow, and without the physiological turmoil or "coloring" that most of us find distinctly unpleasant and wish to avoid. Brian Nichols' actions highlight this truth in two separate events. First, months before either trial, police went to Nichols' home to arrest him for raping Lisa. He chose to escape instead of surrendering. He wedged a file cabinet against a toilet, hoisted himself through a skylight in one of the bathrooms, and climbed onto the roof of the condominium. All the while, the police had his place surrounded and were waiting for a judge to sign the search warrant before forcing their way inside. As Nichols walked across the roof of adjoining units, none of the police officers ever thought to look up, and Nichols escaped. The cunningness required to even attempt such a feat knowing the police were right outside, let alone succeed, speaks volumes about his inability to feel the "coloring" described by Dr. Hare.

Second, if anyone remains unconvinced whether such a fearless or emotionless demeanor was indeed present in Brian Nichols during his crime spree on March 11th, watch the surveillance footage of him exiting the CNN parking deck. It should summarily silence any opposition. The videotape footage shows Nichols as he calmly walked down a set of stairs following the last of the car-jackings. Even though we now know that police sirens were blasting throughout the parking deck, Nichols never seemed to quicken his step or hasten his departure from the garage. Instead, he casually strolled down the steps with his hands in his pockets. He never appeared to be afraid. Neither fear of capture, nor the consequences he would most certainly suffer were his motivation for escaping that day.

It was because of people like Brian Nichols, who display blatant disregard for others, that I set out on a private journey to make sense of such callous behavior. That journey led me to discover the writings of John Locke. I vividly remember when

I discovered the 17th Century English philosopher's theories and writings as a wide-eyed college student at the University of Michigan. Arrogantly nodding in agreement as I read along, I felt as though he understood me and eloquently expressed exactly how I felt. Essentially, he writes of a "Social Contract" each one of us enters into with one another regarding how we will conduct ourselves in society. When we each live up to the terms of that agreement, the whole of society reaps the benefit. It was the idea of a "Social Contract," and prosecuting those who violate it, which ultimately landed me in the Fulton County District Attorney's office and a member of the prosecution team for Brian Nichols. I believe, once you voluntarily, and without justification hurt someone, you have broken the "Social Contract" and should suffer the consequences. Dr. Hare's writings merge with this theory by describing how psychopaths understand the rules of society and the conventional meanings of right and wrong. They are capable of controlling their behavior and are aware of the potential consequences of their actions. Nevertheless, psychopaths choose to disregard society's rules when those rules do not fit their needs. In the opinion of many in the mental health field, psychopaths should be held accountable for their actions, and I whole-heartedly agree.

It was never difficult for me to prosecute even the most heinous crimes. I believed then and now, that if an individual is truthfully accused of committing a crime, they should stand before a jury of their peers and be judged. The whole of society should not be subjected to the repeated poor choices of a putrid few by allowing those offenders to continue to live amongst us. I subscribe to the view that breaking the Contract should result in the individual losing the privilege of being a part of society.

There are those that will question my beliefs and whether I take into account mitigating circumstances in various situations. To those queries, I respond by simply saying, "Yes, I do." There are situations when mitigating circumstances should play an appropriate role in determining the degree of punishment. It was not my calling, however, to determine the cause for people's transgressions upon society, but to bring justice to bear for the wrongs they commit. I leave the former to those who have dedicated their professional lives to resolving the reasons behind those mitigating circumstances.

Dr. Hare writes that many authors on the subject have commented that the shortest chapter in any book on psychopathy should be the one on treatment. A one-sentence conclusion such as "No effective treatment has been found," or, "Nothing works," is the common wrap-up to scholarly reviews of the literature. Such is the case for Brian Nichols. At the time of his arrest for raping Lisa, Nichols held a stockpile of weapons and ammunition in his condominium. That cache of weapons would suggest to most, his willingness to use them whenever he thought necessary. Brian Nichols would have used his own weapons on the morning of March 11th if they had been at his disposal. Nothing exists that would stop him from killing or maiming again if given the chance. Furthermore, nothing he has done since the shootings would suggest any treatment would prevent him from continuing as a threat to society.

As of this writing, Brian Nichols has continued to reveal his manipulative, calculating, and dangerous nature. Since 2005, jail authorities have twice found evidence of Nichols' plans to escape from jail. In his last known attempt, he was discovered asking a female visitor about the exterior of the jail. While she traveled through security gates, barbed-wire fences and guard towers, she explained to him what she saw. He listened and probed further from a jailhouse telephone, unaware or unconcerned the conversation was being recorded. He convinced his accomplice and prison personnel to help him smuggle into the jail large heavy-duty construction equipment strong enough to cut through cinder block walls: all in an effort to escape.

Brian Nichols' own parents know, as I suspect they have for some time, that no treatment exists that will help their son. His condition did not rear its ugly head for the first time on March 11th, nor was its presence a surprise on the day he raped his girlfriend at gunpoint. At the time, I thought it telling that no member of Nichols' immediate family attended either of his rape trials. This was particularly perplexing to me when I learned his father had returned from South Africa to clear Nichols' belongings from the condominium he rented from Lisa. I've seen news articles that indicate his parents' knowledge of his mental state and lack of any effective treatment that stem back at least to the early 90's. His own mother's despair about her son's state is evident in a March 12th e-mail to her friend Deputy Dowdell. In that e-mail, she lamented the following, "Me and Gene are grieving and angry Brian is still alive . . . If he would've killed himself there would be finality. We now have to wait years for the judicial system to execute him." Some say those were merely expressions of a distraught mother, and I agree with that analysis, but for different reasons. When I first learned of that particular e-mail, I questioned the level of pain, hurt, disappointment, anger or any combination thereof, that causes a mother to wish death on her son. By all accounts, they are nice people. They certainly are not the kind one would assume would wish death on their own child. Assuming that to be true, why wish death on your son if not because you know in your heart that he is damaged beyond repair.

During Brian Nichols' trial for murder, I will watch with a pained heart as the survivors recount their stories of his bloody rampage. I will remember my fear and angst for the safety of my wife and children during his 26-hour crime spree. I will recall conversations I had with the victims before their premature deaths, and I will grieve again. I will fight off the nagging thought, which comes less often these days but will never go away, that I bear some responsibility for this tragedy. I will not flinch, however, if a jury decides his punishment is death. Instead, I will view such a decision as the ultimate expulsion from society, and I believe that *should* be the fate of Brian Gene Nichols.

Press release from the Fulton County District Attorney, Paul Howard.

Brian Nichols Indicted on 54 Counts, State Will Seek Death Penalty

Defendant Charged with Murders of Four, Numerous Other Counts Relating to March 11th Incident at Courthouse and After

Atlanta – Fulton County District Attorney Paul L. Howard, Jr. (Atlanta Judicial Circuit) announces that Brian Gene Nichols (33) has been indicted on 54 counts related to the 11 March 2005 killings at the Fulton County Courthouse and while on the run. He is charged with murder (four counts), felony murder (four counts), aggravated assault on a peace officer (three counts), aggravated assault with a deadly weapon (18 counts), aggravated battery (two counts), robbery by force, theft by taking, escape, and hijacking a motor vehicle (five counts). Specifically, he is charged with the murders of Judge Rowland W. Barnes, Ms. Julie Ann Brandau, Sergeant Hoyt Teasley, and Federal Customs Agent David Gary Wilhelm as well as the assault upon Deputy Cynthia Hall and numerous other victims.

The State will seek the death penalty against the defendant.

These charges are merely an accusation, and the defendant is presumed innocent until and unless proven guilty.

WHEN THE CASE IS DEATH

"I believe in the death penalty."

"Justice is itself the great standing policy of civil society; and any eminent departure from it, under any circumstances, lies under the suspicion of being no policy at all."

-Edmund Burke
18th Century Philosopher

ONE of the most emotionally charged issues at the center of the intersection of politics, religion, race, and class in America is the death penalty. If the Prosecution in Nichols' case spends more than five minutes arguing whether his actions meet the legal requirements for the death penalty, time will have been wasted. People may disagree with my position, but no one will argue that the greatest challenge to those selected for this jury is not a legal question, but a philosophical and moral one.

In Georgia, a criminal's actions can qualify him for the death penalty if he meets any one of ten aggravating factors set out in the death penalty statute. By 9:30 A.M. on March 11th, Brian Nichols satisfied five of the qualifiers. After he escaped from custody, he created a great risk of death to more than one person in a public place, and murdered a judicial officer and a peace officer during the exercise of their official duties, simply for the purpose of evading arrest. There is no legitimate question whether he actually committed these acts. Therefore, no legitimate argument that he does not meet the statutory requirements for the death penalty exists. Nevertheless, there are those who would argue that imposing a sentence of death is wrong and cloaking it with the stamp of government authority doesn't change the impropriety of the act.

In my role as a lawyer, I understand those arguments. Still as a man, father, and husband, I am far less objective. If Brian Nichols is sentenced to die, I envision any number of protestors will argue that a sentence of life without parole is a better, more civilized option. I have to believe that those who oppose the death penalty justify their stance not on a case-by-case basis, but oppose it on principle, despite the criminal or the crime. What would they say then to the family of Brian Nichols' next victim? Prior to the morning he decided to rape his ex-girlfriend at gunpoint, he chose to live only in the shadows of illegal activity. Until then he committed, relatively speaking, minor offenses like selling marijuana and frequenting prostitutes. On the morning of August 19, 2004, he crossed over into the spotlight of major felonies. Is there anyone who can honestly say to themselves that they believe he would not kill again if given the opportunity? I venture to say that neither his rape victim nor her family would question whether he would if given the chance. Yet, the ultimate irony is that what I or any of his other victims feel or believe is of no consequence.

No matter on which side of this debate you find yourself, only 12 people will be responsible for deciding Brian Nichols' fate. When I think of the mothers, daughters, husbands, sons, and wives unwillingly pulled into this tragedy, I feel deeply sorry for them. It will not be an easy decision or an enviable position.

People routinely speculate about what course of action they would take in a given situation and offer thoughtless speculation about how they would behave. In conversations at the office or over dinner with friends where the topic is some particularly heinous criminal or their crimes, people cavalierly toss out comments like, "I'd flip the switch with no hesitation." In reality, most of us will go our entire lives without consciously deciding whether a person should live or die. In contrast, we all can relate to situations where we make split-second decisions that *may* have life or death consequences; choosing whether to swerve left into oncoming traffic or right onto the shoulder of a road in order to avoid an accident. Such decisions are easy for most of us to relate to and visualize. That type decision is markedly different from listening to graphic accounts of a murderous rampage, facing the offender, his parents, and the families of his victims, and then deciding whether death will be his punishment. The 12 jurors selected in Fulton County to hear this case will have a taxing job to hold the balance of another's life in their hands. Their collective decision will perhaps become a defining moment in their lives, and at the very least, one they will never forget. They will be forced to confront the core of their belief systems, make a decision of this magnitude based upon it, and then stand before the world to be judged by it.

Whenever I think of the gravity of the jurors' decision, I think of my wife and her stance on the death penalty. She is against it in this case and every other. She has spent her entire professional career fighting for those who lacked the knowledge and resources to fight for themselves. Her stance on the death penalty is an extension of her desire to protect people disproportionately and adversely affected by society. She believes at times, that society callously discards its most vulnerable members. I, however, struggle to understand the complexity of her position in light of the close friends she lost, and how her life would have been shattered completely if not for a difference of approximately five minutes. Had I exited that stairwell on the eighth floor minutes earlier, I would have walked directly into Brian Nichols' path as he fled Judge Barnes' courtroom. He most certainly would have killed me, leaving her a young widow and our children fatherless. Both consequences are too painful for me to dwell on or even discuss with her. Yet, she opposes the death penalty. On some level her stance on the issue speaks volumes about her conviction to her beliefs.

I want people to understand that, for me, this is not merely an attempt to seek vengeance upon Brian Nichols for the carnage he created. Since the shootings, I have never hidden the fact that I was furious with him for what he did, and what he put my family through. My private pain, however, is not why I believe he deserves the death penalty. Instead, I look at the totality of his actions and say he is exactly the kind of criminal for which the death penalty is reserved. There are murders committed every day at alarming rates in Atlanta and around the country. When people finally are charged with those crimes, the district attorneys don't ask for the death penalty in every case. They don't ask in each instance because the death penalty is reserved for those crimes that shock our consciousness and are particularly atrocious.

Nevertheless, the ultimate irony in this entire tragedy is that Brian Nichols claimed to have acted as a soldier on March 11th, fighting back against an oppressive judicial system. Yet, he has already availed himself of an extraordinary array of lawyers at the expense of that same system in an attempt to get the very thing he withheld from all of his shootings victims – the chance to live. The debate on the death penalty will continue long after this case fades from news headlines. It remains to be seen on which side of the issue, *The State of Georgia v. Brian Gene Nichols* will fall – life or death.

Author's Endnote

THERE were times in writing *"Waking the Sleeping Demon"* when I felt less like the architect of this story and more like the riverbed over which this story splashed and flowed as it made its way downstream. It is an awesomely powerful story, and one that demanded to be told exactly as it was, which left little room for a balanced discussion of the death penalty. As I came to the end of my journey in penning *"Waking the Sleeping Demon,"* the lawyer in me felt a responsibility to say more about the disproportionate and unfair administration of the death penalty. The following is not, nor was it intended to be, a thorough examination of the countless number of complex issues that plague death penalty cases across the country. Instead, it is my hope that I have given voice to the other side of the debate in a seemingly unlikely forum. It also was not my intention to convince anyone to change any opinion they hold on the issue. If *"Waking the Sleeping Demon"* and this section spark discussions and force people to re-examine their views, I will have successfully accomplished an important goal. Ultimately, only one matter is certain, and that is determining whether we should keep the death penalty as a viable option is not as clear-cut as it may seem in the case of Brian Nichols.

Critics of the death penalty can point to any number of cases around the country, and indeed the world, which highlight the egregious application of death penalty laws. When they make such arguments, opponents emphasize the arbitrary nature of determining which cases qualify for the death penalty, particularly when comparing capital punishment systems from state to state. In analyzing the issue, they point to race as a significant determining factor for use of the death penalty. According to the Death Penalty Information Center, modern studies consistently show that those who kill white victims are more likely to receive the death penalty than those who kill black victims. Indeed, in 96% of states where there have been reviews of race and the death penalty, there was a pattern of either race-of-victim or race-of-defendant discrimination or both. Brian Nichols' case, however, would not fit into this statistical analysis. Advocates for applying the death penalty in Brian Nichols' case would highlight the fact that although he is black, not all of his victims were white. He did not choose his victims that day based upon their race, and as a result, his race was not a factor in the decision to make this a capital case.

Some opponents argue that by imposing death in certain cases and not in others we, as a society, place a higher value on the lives of certain people over others. Most enlightened people would agree that using race as a factor to determine in which cases to invoke death penalty statutes is inherently wrong. In spite of that, there are times when killing some members of society as opposed to others *should* carry a harsher punishment. On the surface, this may seem a distasteful comment, but, when given critical analysis, the argument is clear. Brian Nichols murdered four people essential to our system of justice. It is that system, for better and for worse, which is the lynchpin of a civilized society. As Americans, we value the freedoms we enjoy and have come to expect such freedoms as a birthright. Whenever those freedoms are trampled upon, we protest loudly and expect that others will listen. We hold the protectors of those freedoms to higher standards, and at times they fall short. Nevertheless, if there is a lack of respect for the system and the people who help to make our streets safe to walk and our homes safe to live in, our society disintegrates into anarchy. Are there really any among us who would choose such chaos as a way of life?

Further, opponents of the death penalty contend that lack of quality legal representation invariably leads to death sentences. After a study of death penalty representation in the South, *The National Law Journal* concluded that capital trials are, "more like a random flip of the coin than a delicate balancing of scales, because the defense attorney is, too often . . . ill-trained, unprepared and grossly underpaid." Even Supreme Court Justices have openly questioned whether some lawyers who defend death penalty cases are effective. "People who are well represented at trial do not get the death penalty. I have yet to see a death case among the dozens coming to the Supreme Court on eve-of-execution stay applications in which the defendant was well represented at trial." Supreme Court Justice Ruth Bader Ginsburg is quoted to have made those comments in her support for a moratorium on the death penalty.

No such argument concerning the lack of superior representation would apply to the case of Brian Nichols. If the estimated cost of over 1.5 million dollars in defense costs is any indication of the quality of his defense, he stands in exclusive company. Additionally, the pedigree for Nichols' lawyers is impressive, with Harvard, Yale, Georgetown, and NYU among them, and these lawyers are not new to the bar. When those schools are mentioned as an afterthought, compared to the breadth of their experience in the highly specialized death penalty area, you are describing a real "dream team." Unfortunately, for other defendants facing capital cases in Georgia, Brian Nichols' defense has drained an already depleted system of resources needed to defend them. The real injustice due to lack of quality legal representation is not presented in the face of Brian Nichols. Rather, it is seen in all the other nameless faces sitting in jails throughout Georgia whose cases won't receive even one lawyer capable of handling their case, let alone a team.

Another reason the subject of the death penalty makes headlines is due to gross miscarriages of justice. Newspaper headlines capture reader's attention and the attending articles detail the facts of cases where an innocent man, or one whose guilt raises troubling questions, sits on death row. Even more appalling are the cases where an innocent person has been executed. Those wrongly convicted or tragically put to death expose the cavernous fault lines in the death penalty system. The case of Larry Griffin is certainly an example of the fallibility of the system. Griffin was convicted in 1981 for killing a man in a drive-by shooting in Missouri, and he was executed in1995. Some ten years later, Prosecutors reopened the case when evidence came to light that not only raised doubts concerning whether Griffin was the shooter, but whether he was even in the area at the time of the shootings. For Larry Griffin, evidence that tended to point toward his innocence rather than guilt came too late. Sadly, we have become accustomed to revelations of DNA tests, or other exculpatory evidence exonerating inmates, and the empty apologies offered to them for their years wasted on death row. Another example of the death penalty systems' failings is the case of Troy Anthony Davis. He was convicted in 1991 for killing an off-duty police officer in Savannah, Georgia. No physical evidence ever connected Davis to the killing. It was only the testimony of eyewitnesses that sealed his fate. Of the nine eyewitnesses, seven have recanted or changed their testimony. At least one did so during the trial, but that fact was not presented to the jury hearing Davis' case. Each of the witnesses offered fear of retaliation from the actual shooter and pressure from the police investigating the case as the reasons for blaming Davis for a killing he did not commit. Unfortunately, the Georgia Supreme Court denied his latest request for a new trial in April 2008. By way of contrast, there is no doubt that

Brian Nichols killed Judge Rowland Barnes, Julie Ann Brandau, Sergeant Hoyt Keith Teasley and FBI Agent David Wilhelm. No doubt whatsoever. Should a jury decide that death is his fate, no amount of time will pass when new evidence might surface that will cast doubt on his culpability for those crimes.

Arguably, the most vexing issue as it relates to the death penalty is dealing with the mentally ill. In 1986, former Supreme Court Justice Thurgood Marshall delivered the opinion of the Court in the case of *Ford v. Wainwright*, concluding that the Eighth Amendment prohibited States from inflicting the death penalty upon a prisoner who is insane.

"The natural abhorrence civilized societies feel at killing one who has no capacity to come to grips with his own conscience or deity is still vivid today. And the intuition that such an execution simply offends humanity is evidently shared across this Nation. Faced with such widespread evidence of a restriction upon sovereign power, this Court is compelled to conclude that the Eighth Amendment prohibits a State from carrying out a sentence of death upon a prisoner who is insane. Whether its aim be to protect the condemned from fear and pain without comfort of understanding, or to protect the dignity of society itself from the barbarity of exacting mindless vengeance, the restriction finds enforcement in the Eight Amendment..."

Notwithstanding that decision, States have continued to grapple with the issue. In January 2007, the Supreme Court decided to revisit the issue of executing mentally ill criminals when it granted the right of review in the case of Scott Panetti, a Texas man ultimately convicted of killing his in-laws. During the trial, where he fired his lawyers and represented himself, Panetti adorned a 1920's era cowboy suit and rambled incoherently about matters unrelated to the trial. Interviewed after the trial, jurors admitted they were afraid of him, and that his antics made them uncomfortable.

Dealing with mental illness within the context of the law is difficult and often controversial. The competing interest of personal responsibility and the reality of mitigating factors stretch our criminal justice system thin when it comes to balancing these oftentimes conflicting notions. Most people would accept the punishment of incarceration in a psychiatric hospital for an individual whose mental illness is beyond reasonable dispute. When thinking about the mentally ill, some conjure up images of disheveled persons who carry on entire conversations with themselves or inanimate objects. Typically, psychopaths do not fit that clichéd image and are not "crazy" as defined by people in general conversations or by accepted legal psychiatric standards. With a chilling inability to treat other people as thinking, feeling human beings, they act on their own selfish impulses with cold, calculating rationality and not from a deranged mind out of control. Attempting to understand this disconnect between such morally incomprehensible behavior, exhibited by a seemingly normal person, has left ordinary people and esteemed scholars equally bewildered. There is little doubt that during the trial Brian Nichols' expert legal team will raise issues of his competence or mental capacity. His seasoned legal team has already disclosed their contention that Nichols suffered from a delusional compulsion at some point during his crime spree.

Under Georgia law, a person is not legally insane simply because he suffers from schizophrenia or a psychosis. Rather, a defendant is not guilty by reason of insanity if, at the time of the criminal act, the defendant did not have the mental capacity to distinguish between right and wrong in relation to such act or a mental disease caused a delusional compulsion that overmastered his will to resist committing the crime.

To assert that Nichols was unable to control his desire to commit the crimes of March 11th borders on the absurd.

Obviously, there is very little material available with which to mount any defense for his actions. There is a vast difference, however, between the Scott Panetti's of the world and the likes of Brian Nichols. Passing Brian Nichols on the street would not bring to mind the image of the "crazy person" depicted in television and films. Still, it would be prudent to avoid him and his violently unpredictable wrath. The stereotypical "crazies," the psychopaths, and those that fall somewhere in between have some form of mental defect. That fact raises the hotly debated question of whether mentally ill persons should ever be subjected to capital punishment.

At some point during the Nichols trial, opponents of the death penalty will argue that using death as a punishment is cruel and will question whether any of us really want to live in a society where an eye is taken for every eye lost. They will posit that there are ways to accomplish the goal of removing dangerous individuals from society without employing barbaric methods of killing them. If, such an argument might continue, society decides to honestly assess and treat the roots of crime, then we are compelled to create more civilized solutions for dealing with the offenders.

Proponents for the death penalty could easily raise the opposite view by asking: *Should we release the incurable and demented upon the prison population to wreak havoc on those civilians charged with keeping its order?* Researchers who have studied psychopaths have tried to identify what makes them tick, and to date, have been unsuccessful in finding a cause or a cure. They have concluded, however, that for psychopaths who commit violent acts, there is a high probability they will become repeat violent offenders. Moreover, psychopaths are not considered mentally ill such that incarceration in a mental facility is a viable option. As a result, we are left only with our prisons to warehouse the likes of Brian Nichols. Admittedly, no qualified professional has diagnosed Brian Nichols as an incurable psychopath, but the phrase, "the most reliable indicator of future behavior is past behavior," inevitably comes to mind when one thinks of him and his crimes.

Other questions come to mind like: *(i) Should a person be medicated forcibly long enough to establish competency in order that they face a capital trial and ultimately death? (ii) If a person is incurable, demented, and dangerous, do we, as a society, wipe them from our midst by killing them? (iii) If legitimate questions arise after a conviction in a capital case, do we ignore the evidence simply because their lawyer failed to present it during the initial trial?* Ask yourself these and other troubling questions when pondering the death penalty. Then ask five other people those same questions. The range of answers received and passions evoked will highlight why people vehemently debate this issue, and why the debate will continue.

AFTERWORD

I T has been over three years since the tragic shootings at the Fulton County Courthouse and victims, as well as some families of other victims, have filed civil lawsuits because of the tragedy. Security protocols have changed. Deputies have been fired or assigned different duties throughout the Courthouse. Yet, Brian Nichols still has not been held accountable for his crimes. Delay, after delay, after delay has plagued this case, and for this there is plenty of blame to dole out between the first presiding Judge, the defense attorneys, and the prosecution. Part of the reason for the setbacks is because Fulton County District Attorney Paul Howard refuses to compromise and accept a guilty plea with a punishment of life in prison. Instead, he continues to insist on pursuing a sentence of death. On the other hand, he has a responsibility to the citizens of Fulton County to restore a sense of order at the Courthouse by pushing for the greatest penalty available. The defense attorneys have exhausted almost two million dollars in public funds preparing Nichols' defense and have not selected their first juror. Some might argue they are merely being prudent advocates for their client by exploring every reasonable defense. Others would argue their actions have been frivolous and wasteful. Judge Hilton Fuller, who some sight as losing control over the case in ways even the judge from the famed O.J. Simpson case would find egregious, voluntarily recused himself from the troubled murder case. Judge Fuller, in a highly questionable move, granted an interview about the case to *The New Yorker* magazine's Jeffrey Toobin, and then stated, "The whole world knows he [Nichols] did it." Both Fuller's decision to grant the interview and the statement violated his duty to remain impartial and dictated he step down as the presiding judge. As a result, Cobb County Superior Court Judge James "Jim" Bodiford stepped in to handle the case. Immediately striking a new tone, Judge Bodiford vowed to hold court on Saturdays in order that the case is concluded by the end of 2008. To the welcomed surprise of many observers, Bodiford forced the defense team to stop hiding behind the veil of a "lack of funds," and set a trial date for July of 2008. Additionally, Judge Bodiford has re-visited other issues. For example, the trial should have been moved from the Courthouse where Nichols' initial crime spree occurred but for numerous reasons was not. Judge Bodiford has agreed to re-visit that issue to ensure a fair trial. Wherever the site of the trial, it will be a difficult task, at best, for lawyers to select an impartial jury in Fulton County. The people of the city of Atlanta will never forget the events of March 11, 2005, and the sooner Brian Nichols is punished for those crimes, the sooner the city can begin to heal.

Acknowledgments

I WOULD first like to thank my husband Tim for his unwavering belief in my ability to write, even before I believed in myself. I would not have done this without you. I also want to thank my girls for watching my every move, and by doing so, motivating me to be the best person I can be and hopefully a positive role model in their lives. To my editor Kim Rouse, thank you for dedicating the time to help me focus my vision and see it through to completion. There is a phrase that says, "A mind once stretched by a new idea, never regains its original dimensions," and I am honored to have worked with you on this journey and look forward to reaching new heights together. To my mom, a.k.a. "*Room 222,*" thank you for everything. Who would ever have thought all of those summer reading assignments and book reports you required of my brothers and me would lead to this! To my father and my brothers, thank you for paving the way for me to navigate uncharted waters while knowing that each of you would answer any distress signal I sent out. To Ash, thank you for trusting me to tell your story, and in the process, offering me the opportunity to live out my dreams.

I am forever grateful. To all of my friends and supporters who, whenever you saw or talked to me, never forgot to offer words of encouragement and support. Your thoughts and well wishes have sustained me in ways no words can describe. Last, but certainly not least, to those individuals who shared your stories from March 11th with me – thank you. Thank you. Thank you.

REFERENCE MATERIALS

Atlanta Journal and Constitution Newspaper Articles.

Baldus, David, et al. 1998. In The Post-Furman Era: An Empirical And Legal Overview, With Recent Findings From Philadelphia, 83 Cornell Law Review, 1638.

Coyle, M., et al. 1990. Fatal Defense: Trial and Error in the Nation's Death Belt. National Law Journal, June 11.

Fulton County Daily Reporter Newspaper Articles.

Kim, Alice. 2002. A Year In Review. The New Abolitionist, Issue 23 Pp. 405-410.

Hare, Robert, PhD. 1993. Without Conscience, The Disturbing World of the Psychopaths Among Us. Pp. 5, 38, 56, 143, 194 – 195.

Marshall, Thurgood, Justice. Ford v. Wainwright, 477 U.S. 399, at 409 -410.

Smith, Ashley and Stacy Mattingly. 2005. Unlikely Angel. Pp. 11 – 17, 85 – 86, 139 -140, 206 – 212, 219 – 220.

Bernes, J., Wallin v. The State, 285 Ga. App. 377 (2007), citing Shepherd v. State, 280 Ga. 245, 248 (1), n. 3 (626 SE2d 96) (2006)

About the Author

As a sixth grader growing up in Akron, Ohio, a teacher asked Shoran Reid what she wanted to be when she grew up. Without hesitation, she told him a lawyer, and then set out on the path to accomplish that goal. After graduating from Miami University in 1991, and The Ohio State University College of Law in 1994, she moved to Atlanta to become a tax lawyer. She practiced with a small law firm before a case fortuitously landed on her desk, which changed the course of her career. Shoran represented an up and coming rap duo at trial and the rush she felt presenting her client's evidence was unparalleled to any professional endeavor she had experienced. The duo became known as the multi-platinum, Grammy Award winning group Outkast, and she enjoyed a nearly decade long career as a successful civil trial attorney. In fact, she loved it so much she would have done it for free. In the meantime, she met her legal match outside of the courtroom and the two married in 1997 and later became parents of two daughters. In the interest of pursuing other opportunities, her husband left his firm, Shoran left the practice of law, and the family moved to Florida. During a nine-month hiatus, Shoran designed a course to train law students on the practical aspects of trail advocacy. Administrators from the cutting-edge law school of Florida Coastal, excited by her ingenuity and drive, hired her on the spot to teach the course. In the semesters that followed, she also taught other courses at the law school including Contracts and Pre-Trial Litigation before embarking on her passion for writing. She began creating her first novel, and then the events of March 11, 2005 occurred and altered her priorities. Instead of writing in between teaching and taking her girls to ballet, she approached researching and writing *"Waking the Sleeping Demon"* with her hallmark determined focus. Currently, she is hard at work on finishing her yet untitled second book.

ABOUT ASHUTOSH "ASH" JOSHI

ASHUTOSH Joshi, known by everyone as "Ash," was born in the small town of Mumbai, India. His parents came to this country when he was only three years old. At an early age, Ash was driven by the desire to exceed his parents' expectations of first generation immigrants and was grounded with a sense of purpose and integrity.

He received his Bachelor of Arts degree from the University of Michigan in 1993 and earned his Juris Doctorate degree from Emory University School of Law in 1996. After graduating from law school, Ash began his legal career in the Fulton County

Public Defenders' office where he defended over 200 clients and tried several capital cases. He then moved over to the Prosecutor's office in Fulton County, and worked as an Assistant District Attorney in the Homicide and Crimes Against Women and Children Unit. Ash successfully prosecuted over 100 cases, several dealing with rape and child molestation. It was in his role as prosecutor in the Brian Nichols rape trial and subsequent courthouse shootings which made Ash Joshi a household name. He recently shared his story in prosecuting the Nichols case with his longtime friend and writer, Shoran Reid, who has penned a book on his life-changing experience.

Ash's extensive trial experience has garnered him a reputation as a nationally recognized criminal defense commentator, and he has appeared on Fox News and MSNBC as a legal expert. Ash is the founder of The Joshi Law firm and continues to employ his tenacious defense strategies to represent high-profile clients. He is admitted to practice in the State of Georgia and the United States District Court for the Northern District of Georgia. He and his wife Suparna, reside in Atlanta with their two children.